MW00612848

MUSINGS ON A BALANCING ACT VOLUME 1

Essays on Competition Obedience

Adele Yunck
Cover illustration by
Kimberly Hundley
Other illustrations by
Adele Yunck

JABBY Productions

Copyright © 2021 Adele Yunck

Musings On A Balancing Act Volume 1
Essays on Competition Obedience
By Adele Yunck
Cover illustration by Kimberly Hundley
Other illustrations by Adele Yunck

Published by:

JABBY Productions
3676 W. Ellsworth Rd.
Ann Arbor, MI 48103
https://www.northfielddogtraining.com/

Copyright ©2021 by Adele Yunck

All rights reserved. No part of this book may be reproduced or transmitted in any form or by any means, electronically or mechanically, including photocopying, recording, or by any information storage or retrieval system, except in the case of brief excerpts quoted in reviews, without written permission from the author or publisher.

First Edition 2021

ISBN: 978-0-9664574-6-9

To Fritz
For your on-going support and your mad editing skills

CONTENTS

INTRODUCTION

I n 2008, right after judging an outdoor Rally trial, I started writing essays about competition obedience and sharing them on my blog. My first essay was entitled "Musings on Entering the Ring". Over the next several years, I wrote a series of obedience-related essays. This book is a collection of about half of what I wrote back then, with updates and additions, and even a new one. They are a mixture of stories and how-to, filling in some gaps left by my two books, Competition Obedience: A Balancing Act, co-written with Judy Byron, and The Art of Proofing. I hope you find them useful and fun to read.

As Judy Byron and I wrote at the beginning of *Competition Obedience: A Balancing Act*, we referred to handlers as "she" and dogs as "he" throughout the book to simplify our writing. I've continued that tradition here. As before, I mean no disrespect for male handlers with female dogs!

In the e-book version of this book, I used quite a few links throughout the text. Rather than expect you to type those in, I've created a webpage with those links, which you can find here:

https://www.northfielddogtraining.com/MOABAV1/links.php

I hope you find that webpage helpful.

Adele Yunck
February 2021

1. CRUCIAL FOUNDATION EXERCISES

This is a list of what I consider crucial foundation exercises to teach a new puppy or young dog that you plan to show in obedience or rally. In reviewing the detailed training logs I kept when first training my Flat-Coated Retriever Sonic, I learned that by the time she was 4 months old, she had a good start on all of these exercises plus some other field-related ones. This is not meant to be a "how to" guide but rather to show you why I think these are important exercises.

Follow the cookie

This skill is important because I use a treat in my hand as a lure to initiate quite a few of my foundation exercises. If your puppy is lunging and biting obnoxiously to grab the treat, it isn't any fun for you. Who wants to get their hand and fingers munched on? You need to teach your puppy the skill of politely following the lure. Pushing the food into your puppy's nose instead of pulling away can help reduce his lunging for the food. I view the treat in my hand like a magnet - if it gets too far from my puppy's nose, the treat loses its power. When first teaching my puppy to follow food, I move the food at a slow enough speed that my puppy can keep up with my movement.

Voluntary attention

I use "structured shaping" when beginning to teach my puppy attention, which means I assume a specific posture when starting to work on the exercise. I get my puppy into a sit, and then move myself into the desired position in relation to my puppy. Once I'm in the position, either with my puppy in front of me or in heel position, I wait for voluntary attention. Voluntary means that I do my best to remain silent and let my puppy figure out that looking at me is beneficial. I initially want my puppy to look at something other than my hands, which are holding treats. My long-term goal is for my puppy to make eye contact when in front, and to focus on some spot on my left side when in heel position. The exact spot on your left side will depend on the size of your dog and your height. For my Flat-Coated Retrievers, they are looking up toward the side of my head or my left shoulder and my terriers tend to focus more on my left hip area.

Position changes

There are three positions that I need my dog to do in competitions (sit, down, stand) and six position changes, i.e., moving from one position into one of the other two positions. Because I want my puppy to learn to use his body in a very specific way for each change of position, I begin all of these with a food lure. My overall goal is that my dog remains in place when doing his position changes so he doesn't creep toward me as the distance between us increases.

One of my students made these very useful observations:

> When working on Sit to Stand and Stand to Sit, I want my dog's front paws to remain in place, while the rear paws move into the new position.

> When working on the Stand to Down and Down to Stand,

I aim for *no* paw movement at all. This takes a fair bit of body control, which many young dogs lack, so don't be discouraged if you don't see this at first.

When working on the Sit to Down and Down to Sit, I like my dog's rear end to remain in place while the front paws move. Some trainers work to have the front stay in place for the Sit to Down.

Find Heel and Distraction Resistance

Initially, this is simply a voluntary and likely-to-be-lured 'get to heel position' exercise. As soon as my puppy understands that getting there is a rewardable action, I add distractions. This teaches my puppy the foundation of *distraction resistance,* by which I mean learning to ignore distractions.

In class, I do increasingly devious actions to pull young dogs away from their owners. The owner turns and ideally runs away from their distracted dog, while I become boring as soon as the dog shows interest in me. The combination of the distraction getting less attractive and the owner running away usually gets the dog chasing after the owner. The dogs learn remarkably quickly to resist strong distractions from me.

Cookie-Toss Recalls

If you think about all of the exercises in Open, four of the seven exercises (Drop on Recall, both retrieves and the Broad Jump) have a recall component. *All* of the Utility exercises have a recall component. You don't want to have to think about recall speed when you are working on the advanced exercises, so make that something for which you lay a very solid foundation. Puppies love the Cookie-Toss Recall exercise, and it lays a great foundation not only for speed but for "grab something (the cookie here), spin around and race back", a valuable component of an excellent retrieve.

Cookie-Toss Down

A quick down from a stand, ideally a fold-back down, is critical for excellent Drop on Recall, Command Discrimination, and Signal Exercises. The Cookie-Toss Down builds a solid understanding of the down and most puppies really love it.

Retrieve

Retrieving is a critical component of the Open and Utility classes. For many people, lack of success when trying to teach their dog to retrieve means not being able to go on beyond the Novice obedience level. Soon after I bring a puppy home, I get started with a play retrieve and the beginnings of the formal retrieve. This includes nose touches to the item, a voluntary take of the item, a hold of the item, and head and collar holds without the dumbbell.

Basic Sit Stay & Impulse control

I love to start puppies with Chris Bach's *sit and maintain* exercise. It teaches puppies that voluntarily offering a sit stay is rewarded. It is also the start of impulse control. When I used to teach Puppy Kindergarten classes, I would ask for an active puppy to demo how to start the exercise. One who jumped up a lot was especially useful. First, I loaded my hand with 5-6 treats. I would get the puppy to sit, and then immediately start using my marker word followed by a quick treat. I basically fed treats as rapidly as the puppy could eat them. When I'd done 3-6 repetitions of this, I would use my release command and turn away from the puppy. I would *only* feed the puppy while he was sitting still. After the release, I'd reload my treats, get the puppy to sit and resume the Yes/treat 3-6 times. Often, after just 2-3 sets of this, the puppy would run around in front of me and offer a sit stay.

Target Marking

I teach puppies to stare at a cookie on a plastic lid, AKA a target, starting from 2-3 feet away. I refer to this as *marking*. Marking is important for the go-out portion of the Utility *Directed Jumping* exercise, the *Directed Retrieve* in Utility, the dumbbell retrieves to a lesser extent, as well as a few other beginnings of exercises. It is also a precursor to teaching a foot touch to a target. I learned the importance of building this foundation step early from my writing partner Judy Byron, before attention to the handler is so strong that the dog doesn't want to look away.

Spins Left and Right

This is an extension of the *Follow the Cookie* game, and it is a wonderful physical warm up for dogs. Teaching your dog to spin in both directions helps to maintain body balance. The spin to the left (counterclockwise) is useful for encouraging a dog who works with his rear out too far to your left to straighten himself up. It is also helpful for the left finish. In Rally Master, there are several signs that require the dog to be able to spin each direction while in heel position.

Platforms

I use platforms - elevated rectangles, ultimately sized just wide enough for my dog to sit straight - for many exercises, including fronts, finishes, sit stays, and go-outs. Your platform can be made from various materials. I have some made of wood with small pieces of 2 x 4 on the bottom for feet, with a top layer of leftover rubber matting from my training building flooring. I've made others from ridged foam insulation, though dog toenails create a lot of divots. I've also made some with a layer of wood sandwiched between rectangles of puzzle-piece foam tile or yoga mats. I consider platforms to be so important that I introduce them to my litters of puppies. They loved climbing on and off them in their puppy pen.

Play Running

This teaches the dog that running with you is fun. While I'd say 90% of my students' dogs don't need a lot of encouragement to charge ahead when their owner starts to run, for the 10% that are pokey, this is a very important exercise. It is a precursor to the *Fast* in obedience heeling.

Maneuvers and Set ups

These teach the dog to move in all directions in relation to you - forward, right, left, backward, tight circle to right, tight circle to left. *Set-ups* are applied maneuvers, and mean getting the dog to move into a sit in heel position, which you need for almost every obedience exercise.

Foot Touch to a Target

I use this primarily for go-outs, but you can also use it for the Broad Jump and the Drop on Recall. It is a great example of an exercise in which the dog learns to move away from the food to get the food. You are holding the food, and your dog needs to move away from you and the food and go touch the target. You use your marker word as he hits the target, and then either the dog returns to you for the treat, you toss a treat away from the target, or you go to him to give it to him. The target can be a plastic lid; a stanchion that is used to support baby gates that make up obedience rings at trials; a rubber feed tub (4-quart size is great for medium to large dogs); a small bath rug or towel; a Post-it note, etc.

Nose Touch to Your Hand

I use this primarily as a release when I'm training or between exercises in the ring. It is also useful when teaching your dog to wrap tightly around you, such as on about turns and the right circle of the Figure 8.

Rhythm Heeling

To me, *Rhythm Heeling* is the most important heeling exercise there is! There are no turns, no pace changes, and no halts with this exercise. It is simply you maintaining a brisk walking rhythm and your dog moving, ideally in a trot, with his attention on you and in correct heel position. A typical heeling pattern lasts for only 30-45 seconds, and yet many, many people struggle to keep their dog actively engaged for an entire pattern. Rhythm Heeling starts with 2-3 steps of moving attention, and gradually, through regular and consistent practice, becomes a lovely dance.

* * *

There you have it. Once your dog is fluent at all of these exercises, you will be well on your way to building a fantastic competition partner.

2. THE ART OF PRAISE & PLAY

I first wrote this essay after I had read the previous month's wonderful, new, glossy-paper issue of Front & Finish magazine, in which there were several articles discussing how to avoid the trap that using food to train your dog can create. It's not that training with food is bad; it's how some trainers use food that is the problem, such as failing to wean away from excessive food; counting on the food to produce the performance that they like and want from their dog, handing out a treat for a really lousy effort on the part of the dog, failing to build a solid relationship with the dog that is separate from treats, etc. Here were all of these articles in the same issue, addressing a topic near and dear to my heart.

This got me thinking about and paying attention to how much food I was using while training the three dogs I was working. They were Gryffin, my 5-year-old neutered male Flat-Coated Retriever, who had 4 UDX legs and 51 OTCh points; Ty, my 3-year-old intact female Flat-Coated Retriever, who just finished her CD; and Joker, a 7-year-old neutered male Border Terrier that we purchased as a pet for our son when said son was 12. Since said son was off at college and his dog loved to train, Joker got to play some, too. I was looking for Open legs on him.

The Flat-Coats were both fanatical retrievers, so I used toys a fair amount in my training in addition to food. Flat-Coated Retrievers are supposed to have a wagging tail; the breed standard says so :-). Having a tail-wagging FCR isn't such a surprise. But Gryff wagged when he sat in front of me. He wagged on his finishes. Almost anytime he sat during training, his tail was sweeping the floor. If it was still, I could usually get it moving with some praise.

Joker the Border Terrier loved treats – I have yet to meet a Border Terrier that doesn't – but he also seemed to be overjoyed at the chance to Do Something and get attention and petting. He loved to leap in the air to touch his nose to my palm. When I praised him and patted him, his tail wagged, his body wiggled, and his facial expression seemed to say, "This is just the best!" It was sure reinforcing to me when he responded this way and it made our training time together fun.

One of the topics I encourage my beginning students to explore is how their dog likes to be praised and/or petted. I think it is important to find out through trial and error what works to calm your dog, as well as what excites him. This is ideally something you do without involving lots of cookies. Some dogs are calmed by a stroke on their head. Others get excited by this. When I was showing my Border Terrier Java in Novice, I got in the habit of bending down and patting him gently on his left side before the start of the Heel Free exercise. If I did that with Ty, she immediately released herself and wiggled all over. She quickly taught me that patting her right before the start of an exercise in the ring was just plain dumb. Instead, I used some quiet praise to let her know I liked the setup she had just done.

About the closest thing to cuddling Gryffin could do was when he was sitting in heel position. I reached down and quietly stroked him on the top of his head or scratched him around his left ear. It helped to calm him some, which was useful, as he tended to be pretty keyed up in the ring. He loved to walk through my legs, front to rear, so I could scratch him in front of his tail, on the top of his rear end. I could do this very rapidly in the ring, especially in Utility when articles or gloves were being picked up by a ring steward. I would then proceed promptly to the location of the next exercise.

Some dogs enjoy it if you pinch their butt. Others hate it. Some like to have you play-grab at their feet. Others are offended by this. Try a variety of what I call "pushy-shovey" games to find out what works with your dog and what doesn't. Some dogs are fickle enough to like something one day and be irritated by it the next. Java was like that. He forced me to try something new frequently.

I had a student whose dog did *not* enjoy petting. Instead, she taught him a "high five" that she would use between exercises when in the ring, which he did enjoy.

I'd also suggest that you simply stand with your hands off your dog and praise him. How does he react? Does he wag his tail? Do his eyes brighten? Or does he ignore you and wander away? Obviously, different dogs and different breeds will react in a variety of ways to praise. Our first two Border Terriers reacted differently from each other. Java was always the most serious of our dogs. It took more effort on my part to get him to cut loose and really wag his tail. Joker definitely lived up to his name and was generally sillier than Java. Our current Border, Jaguar, is somewhere in between.

Many years ago, I was working with someone in a private lesson. When she released her dog, she would grab at the dog's face. Based on how her dog reacted – backing away and trying to avoid the grabbing – the dog found this unpleasant. I took her dog to experiment some with different types of play and releasing. When I gently pinched and prodded the dog in the ribs, she bounced back in an upbeat sort of way. The rib prodding energized her. The head grabbing did not. When the dog's owner changed how she released and played with her dog, her dog responded by bouncing back and interacting instead of avoiding her owner.

In my essay Musings on Entering the Ring, I talked about the Setup Game (which I now call the *Get Readies* game), where you practice moving around your training area, working toward getting your dog to sit in heel position promptly and correctly on the first try. Mix this game with praising and releasing your dog. After a smartly done set up, praise with enthusiasm, give your dog a little push away from you (or a big one, if he likes it), and dash off to the next set up spot. If your dog likes to spin, cue him to do so, and race away and get him to chase you.

I also use a nose touch to my left palm as a release. Java's willingness, or lack thereof, to jump up and touch my hand was usually an indicator of the level of effort he was likely to put forth on the exercise that followed. I learned that with him, lack of effort on the hop required me to correct him with a collar lift.

❄ ❄ ❄

It always strikes me as oxymoronish to say, "Work at playing with your dog," but sometimes that's what it takes. Keep experimenting. If you've tried something for a while and you aren't seeing an improved response from your dog, try something else. Have fun and eventually, so will your dog.

3. THE ART AND SCIENCE OF CORRECTIONS

There are many different ways to teach a dog a given exercise. In general, I believe that showing my dog where he should be or how he should move by using food is the easiest way to teach many exercises. Then, once my dog has a good understanding of the exercise, I introduce corrections to build reliability and to build in an "I Have To" aspect in my dogs. A **correction** is any adjustment, typically physical, which creates the action you want when your dog has failed to respond in the desired way. If you are going to use physical corrections, it is vital that you teach your dog how you want him to respond when you apply that correction.

It is up to you to decide what is the best training method for you and your dog. Some dogs have a very "soft" temperament and you must be very careful about how you use physical corrections. Too much can make them wilt or give up. However, there are clever dogs that learn that "looking pitiful" is the best way to get their trainer to stop making corrections. Other dogs have a very "tough" temperament – they are often also independent – and they require a much firmer hand to get reliability. Sometimes, it is the trainer who has a soft temperament. It is harder for this type of trainer to correct their dog.

When I was first training dogs, using food in training was still a fairly new technique. In that era, many dogs were trained using The Koehler Method or an offshoot of it, which involved choke collars and 6-foot leashes. My friend and writing partner Judy Byron called this the *Jerk and Puke method.* When the correction-based methods are applied by a skilled trainer, they can be very effective and efficient, but when applied poorly with bad timing by an inexperienced trainer, they often produce a dog that lags behind their handler with a tucked tail and poor attitude.

Reinforcement Training

We all learn via reinforcement. A *reinforcer* is any stimulus (an item or an event) that causes a behavior to *increase.* An item might include a treat or toy. An event might include petting or the chance to go out a door. There are positive and negative reinforcers. A positive reinforcer *immediately follows* a correct response, such as giving a treat to a dog right after he comes to you. You are *adding* something desirable after your dog responds. A negative reinforcer *precedes* a response, such as a jerk on a leash that causes your dog to come. You stop the leash jerking, i.e., *take away* something unpleasant, the instant your dog starts to respond. If your timing of the reinforcer is wrong, usually too late, whether positive or negative, your results will not be what you want. For example, you are teaching your dog to sit. He sits and you dig around in your pocket for a treat. You finally produce one and give it to him, but by the time you do, he is standing instead of sitting. Instead of reinforcing a sit, you have just reinforced a stand.

A stimulus is truly a reinforcer only if it causes a behavior to increase. For most dogs, food is a successful and useful positive reinforcer, but if the dog doesn't like a particular treat, it won't work to reinforce his behaviors.

Some dogs work for any kind of food, even if they've just finished a meal. Others require a more careful selection of treats. Switching to a food that your dog likes better or training him when he is hungry will often dramatically improve his responses. I've seen this in my classes numerous times over the many years I've been teaching: a dog is disinterested in his owner's attempt to engage him. I give the trainer some of my more-interesting (often smellier) treats and suddenly their dog is not only interested but sparkling with focus on their trainer.

Punishment Training

The technical meaning of a **punisher** is anything that *decreases* a behavior. Just as there are both positive and negative reinforcers, there are also positive and negative punishers. Using a *positive punisher* means you are *adding* something unpleasant in order to decrease a behavior. A spritz of water in the face to stop barking is a common positive punisher. Using a *negative punisher* means you are *taking away* something desirable or removing privileges to decrease a behavior. An example of a negative punisher is crating your dog when he barks excessively (you are taking away his freedom). If the unwanted behavior is not decreasing, the punisher isn't working.

Why Use Corrections?

I believe that adding corrections is a necessary part of building reliability for the trial ring as well as for life with our dogs, but adding them improperly can create a poor attitude in your dog. A *correction* is any adjustment, typically physical, which creates the action you want when your dog has failed to respond in the desired way. It can be something as gentle as folding the dog's back legs under him to help him sit, a small pop on the leash in the direction you want the dog to move, or an ear pinch for failure to retrieve. Negative reinforcement corrections do not have to be severe and should always increase the quality of the desired behavior.

I do not add a correction to a command until I am reasonably sure my dog understands that command and makes a choice to not respond. Before talking about the technical aspects of how I correct my dogs, I first want to discuss the two different reasons for adding corrections.

First, I want to **decrease** certain behavior, such as jumping on people. That means I want to *punish* the behavior. Generally, when I want to suppress something my dog is doing, especially potentially dangerous activities such as bolting out a door or counter surfing, I use a big and dramatic correction, because I want to have to use it as infrequently as possible.

Years ago, a friend was visiting with her dog, who she had adopted from a local shelter. He was probably a stray because he easily jumped over her 4-foot fence. He was frequently hopping over the baby gate we set up to keep our dogs out of our living room. I happened to catch him in mid-air when he was starting to hop over the gate. I hollered "No!" dramatically at him, grabbed him by the scruff and pushed him back to the dog side. I don't think he ever tried to jump over that gate again.

Another example: when our Flat-Coated Retriever Gryffin was about 5 months old, he would stick his head into our dishwasher every time I'd open the door. I would give him a verbal correction, which made him stop for the moment, but it wasn't suppressing the behavior. I finally realized I was nagging him, but not punishing him. With that in mind, the next time he started to stick his head in the dishwasher, I hollered and doused him with the sink sprayer I happened to be using. That one correction essentially eliminated the "stick his head in the dishwasher" behavior for the rest of his life. It also translated the corrective value to a spray bottle of water – I could give someone a spray bottle of water if Gryffin was annoying them, and he would then leave that person alone.

The other reason I would use corrections is that I want to **in-**

crease the reliability and speed of my dog's response to a command. That means I want to *reinforce* the behavior. When I add a correction that is a negative reinforcer to a behavior, I want to use the mildest force to which my dog will respond. However, if I keep using light corrections and my dog isn't responding any better, then I am nagging.

Silence is Golden

It is essential that you precede any physical correction with a cue, i.e., a verbal command or hand signal. This is so important that I'll say it again: **It is essential that you precede any physical correction with a cue.** Silence in the trial ring should mean, "You are doing the right thing. Keep it up!" rather than "Look out, I may jerk your collar any time now!" Trainers often overlook this important point. When you physically correct your dog from silence, you teach him to mistrust silence.

I learned a useful analogy from Gary Wilkes a zillion years ago: if I was going to come up behind you and whack you with a broom, when would you like me to say "Duck!"? Before, during, or after the whack? I know if someone was doing this to me and was not giving me fair warning, i.e., saying "Duck!" before whacking me, at the very least it would make me upset or even angry with the swinger of the broom. Taken to an extreme, repeated and unavoidable corrections can create *learned helplessness.* To apply this analogy to training your dog, if you start heeling with your dog by jerking the leash forward and *then* saying "Heel!", you aren't giving him any useful information before you jerk on the leash. If you say heel first, he has a small amount of time to react and actually move forward with you before you jerk the leash. He has a chance to *avoid* the correction.

Escape and Avoidance Training

This is the stage in training when your dog learns that he must obey a given command or face the consequence, i.e., a correction. You are conditioning respect into your cue. I do not begin this stage until I have taught the exercise with positive reinforcement.

In the *escape phase*, you give a command and then a physical correction before your dog has a chance to respond. By responding, he *escapes* any further correction. The correction is *negative reinforcement*. He learns that there is a choice he can make.

In subsequent repetitions, your dog *avoids* the correction altogether by responding promptly. It is extremely important to positively reinforce this effort with food or play. From this training, your dog learns he has control over his actions and can predict and understand yours. This process builds trust.

As a rule, I do *not* give food during the escape phase. Immediately after a correction, I verbally praise my dog for the desired behavior, but my use of food should be a clear signal to him that his performance is correct or improved. Instead of giving a treat after a correction, immediately give your dog another chance to do it right without a correction. This is the *avoidance* stage. This effort earns a treat. If you start with the mildest correction, followed immediately by lots of praise, most dogs learn how to respond to the correction and do not lose confidence.

The Art of Corrections

By *the Art of Corrections*, I mean knowing when it is appropriate to correct your dog and when it is not. There is really only one reason to correct your dog: **his lack of effort to comply with a known command**. If your dog is doing something, just the wrong thing, that is often called an "effort error". I certainly verbally interrupt my dog to let him know he's made a wrong choice, but I don't want to use a strong correction to suppress that response, as it may well be something that I want him to do, just not right now.

You must also not correct a dog who is confused. If you are not sure if your dog is confused or just not making effort, I would suggest erring on the side of your dog and assume he is confused. This is part of the art of using corrections. It is important to keep in mind your dog's temperament and how he usually responds when he doesn't understand what he should do. Some dogs freeze up naturally in the face of stress and some mild physical help may be needed to get them moving again.

Types of Corrections

You must temper physical corrections to fit your dog's temperament and size. Sometimes changing collars, say from a buckle to a martingale collar or a pinch collar, can make a radical difference in your dog's response to your corrections.

When using a correction that is intended to motivate your dog to action (a negative reinforcer), start with a mild correction, like a light tug on a buckle collar. Increase the level of correction as necessary until you find the right level for your dog. Don't get into "nagging," which means using frequent, insignificant corrections that don't change your dog's performance.

A negative reinforcement correction should motivate your dog to action, not shut him down. You should see sharper focus, better attitude, and a decrease in response time from your dog.

If your dog's behavior is not increasing after you add a correction, the correction is not working as a reinforcer. If his behavior has decreased after the correction, the correction is serving as a punisher.

Praise should immediately follow your correction. This is extremely important! Do not make corrections in anger. Cultivate a playful attitude about corrections: "Whoops, I gotcha! Let's try again." If you find your dog quits after a correction, help him or review the teaching steps.

Motivational Pops – Beat the Pop

When I say "add a leash correction", I mean that I use a quick leash pop with a release as a correction - the strength of the pop appropriate to the dog's temperament, size, type of collar, etc. - enough to motivate my dog to try harder so he can avoid it the next time, but not so much it makes him give up. A **motivational pop** is a small pop on a dog's collar, whether with your hand in his collar or via a leash. It is intended to motivate him to move faster or try harder, and, though mild, it is a correction. A common student complaint is "I can't use corrections because they shut my dog down." Some dogs actually train their handlers to use no corrections because the dog puts on such a great "Oh, poor me!" act. Certainly, there are dogs that you should avoid correcting physically, but most dogs can learn to move to avoid a mild collar pop.

I teach the motivational pop as an extension of the Hop, so I recommend you wait to introduce the motivational pop until your dog is reasonably adept at the Hop exercise. If you haven't taught the Hop, it is simply the dog starting in a sit, then driving up to a treat in your hand. With a young dog, I want him to keep his rear paws on the floor to lessen the chance of him hurting himself. I start to teach the Hop with a treat in my right hand, then switch the treat to my left hand when I shift so my dog is in heel position.

To teach a motivational pop, position your dog as you did when teaching Hop, with you facing his right side. Warm your dog up with a few hops, then put your left hand in his buckle collar, fingers positioned under the collar from the back to the front. Don't do this with a prong collar on! It would be unpleasant for both of you. Without exerting *any* pressure on his collar, cue a hop. Don't be surprised if he hesitates at first. In fact, even if your dog normally leaps a foot or more in the air, present your treat hand nearer to his nose when you add your hand in his collar. Do this several times, gradually asking for a higher leap. Some dogs appear incapable of moving at all when you take hold of their collar, so you may need to really "go back to kindergarten" with this type of dog.

Once that is smoothed out, the next step is to add a small collar pop up and forward to the hop. I want your dog to learn to move when you tug on his collar. At first, add this tug just before the highest point of your dog's hop, and only do it every 2-3 hops. Gradually, tug earlier and earlier, until it is *just* after your Hop cue. Mark the top of the leap and give the treat from your right hand. You are teaching your dog to move forward and up to relieve the collar pressure and eventually to *beat the pop*. Done carefully, you should start to feel your dog lifting your hand that is holding his collar instead of you lifting him. This becomes a **bounce**. Gradually, your tug comes closer and closer to your verbal hop cue, until the tug is just after your cue.

The Rule of Three

Once your dog understands how to avoid the collar pop by hopping or bouncing promptly, you will be able to use this collar pop to correct a slow heel start, an attention goof, and any place your dog isn't putting forth good effort. I use this collar pop in various ways, especially to motivate my dog to try harder when he's being inattentive or lazy.

Let's say your dog has a consistent problem on heeling, such as going wide on about turns. I assume you've taught the dog where he should be and that you are doing appropriate and accurate footwork on a consistent basis, but he still goes wide regularly. To address this, I use what I call *The Rule of Three*. I add a leash correction to the about turn in this way:
1) As I start into the about turn, I use my verbal cue (close), followed by a leash pop in the direction I need him to move in order to be correct, so a pop across the front of my body, left to right, followed by praise. I might also release after the leash pop if this is very new for my dog. So, Step 1 is **CUE, CORRECT, [dog responds], PRAISE, RELEASE (if appropriate)**.
2A) I immediately try the about turn again, ideally going back to the spot where I just corrected my dog. I use my verbal cue again,

but NO leash pop, followed by praise if there is improvement, followed by a treat. So, Step 2A is **CUE, [dog responds, hopefully with some improvement], PRAISE, TREAT.**

2B) Use this step instead of 2A when you want to go on to step 3 in the same session. I immediately try the about turn again, ideally going back to where I just did the correction. I use my verbal cue again, but NO leash pop, followed by praise if there is improvement. So, Step 2B is **CUE, [dog responds], PRAISE.**

3) Repeat the about turn for a 3rd time, again ideally in the location where you gave the correction on the about turn, do the about turn with NO verbal cue and NO leash pop. In other words, like you would do it in the ring: silently. As soon as you complete the turn, praise, treat if you see improvement, and release. So, Step 3 is **DO THE SKILL IN SILENCE, PRAISE, TREAT, RELEASE.**

Something else I see people struggle with when learning how to use leash corrections fairly: they correct their dog, but then immediately make the task easier. What I prefer to do is try Step 2A first - I want to see if my dog learned anything from my correction in Step 1. What I view as a correction may not be considered a correction by my dog. If my dog does indeed show improvement - do remember he doesn't have to be perfect right away! - then that tells me the correction was appropriate. If your dog responds just as poorly as before, then the correction wasn't sufficient OR the environment is too distracting for your dog's current level of training OR the dog just doesn't understand his job yet. This is when it is crucial to be honest about what your dog understands, and is the art of applying corrections. Most dogs require a lot of repetitions before they really understand how to respond properly to your cues. If you haven't put in the training time to get in the repetitions, be honest and spend more time on your teaching homework before making it harder or adding leash corrections.

To summarize The Rule of Three:
1) CUE, CORRECT, [dog responds], PRAISE, RELEASE (if appropri-

ate)
2A) CUE, [dog responds, hopefully with some improvement], PRAISE, TREAT
2B) CUE, [dog responds], PRAISE
3) DO THE SKILL IN SILENCE, PRAISE, TREAT, RELEASE

In Conclusion

As you prepare to show your dog, it is important to keep in mind how often you have to correct a particular exercise. If it is frequent, be honest with yourself and don't put your dog into a trial situation until you only rarely need to correct it. Dogs can become "ring wise" when shown too soon, which means they learn that you aren't going to fix certain errors when in the ring.

There are times that, try as you might, you are not able to reproduce in training an error that your dog makes in the trial ring. Sometimes, a gentle interruption in the ring is what it takes to stop the dog from making a particular error. You do run the risk of having a judge excuse you for training in the ring, but sometimes, it is a worthwhile risk. If your dog has been doing automatic finishes, a reminder to sit or a step to body block them one time in the ring may be all it takes to prevent it from happening in the future, or at least to greatly reduce the frequency of the goof.

✳ ✳ ✳

In my opinion, adding some level of correction for lack of effort is an important step to take before you show your dog. Be fair and be consistent.

4. SETTING TRAINING GOALS

Anyone who knows me well knows that I am a goal-setter. I wouldn't have the training building, AKA The Big Building, in my back yard if I wasn't. My dogs wouldn't have numerous advanced titles, nor would we have attended the many obedience tournaments and National Specialties that we have over the years, nor would I have finished several other long-term projects – books, DVDs, and running 10Ks. Although goal setting is not for everyone, it is for me, and I'd like to share some of how I use goals to achieve what I have with my dogs in the various title-earning venues in which I've participated.

One of the wonderful aspects of obedience is the title progression. While there are certainly success stories of someone finishing an OTCh (Obedience Trial Champion) title in 2-3 weekends, this is far from the norm. For most of us, getting to a UD (Utility Dog) title or beyond is a multiple-year project.

When I am helping someone new, I like to ask her what goals she is aiming for with her dog. If she hasn't titled a dog before, this will be harder for her to answer, but I like to know what would satisfy her in terms of a title level and a score level. Say she tells me that she would like to earn a CD on her 7-year-old Golden Retriever and she would be thrilled to get scores above 190. Since she's starting with a middle-aged (or beyond) dog, and she hasn't done a lot of training, getting this particular dog trained all the way to the Utility level probably isn't a realistic goal because of the dog's age. So, we concentrate on the Novice exercises and work on her handling so that she's not losing points for handler errors. We work to eliminate as many substantial deductions (those of 3 points or more) as possible, but don't focus as much on the little errors. We might introduce the retrieve and jumping if the dog is physically able to, to add some variety and spice to their training.

If someone comes to me with their new puppy and tells me their goal is an OTCh title, my first and foremost goal is to help them build a very strong foundation with attention to critical details, including solid attention, excellent heeling, accurate position changes, solid stays, fast recalls, and retrieving and jumping skills. While I do stress these details in my early competition classes, not everyone tunes into them, nor is everyone interested in these exacting details. It does take a certain personality of trainer to want to spend time on those details.

I set four different kinds of goals with my dogs: lifetime, annual, monthly, and weekly. Sometimes I write them down, sometimes they are just a flexible list in my head. I do try to revisit these goals regularly to revise as needed.

Lifetime Goals
What titles do I hope to earn during this dog's lifetime?

These are the dream big, shoot-for-the-moon goals. These might be goals that you want to share only with yourself and your best friend, but it really helps if you share these with your instructor!

If my dog is of good quality for his breed, an AKC breed championship is one of my goals. When I get a new dog, I aim for obedience titles of OTCh (Obedience Trial Championship, a title I've earned on 4 Flat-Coated Retrievers and 3 terriers to date) and a UDX (Utility Dog eXcellent). While I haven't achieved one – yet –

I also aim for the Obedience Grand Master title. I was working my way toward that goal with Sonic when the COVID-19 pandemic hit, essentially ending her career. With my seven most recent obedience title-earners, they first earned AKC Rally titles. In the past, I've earned Tracking Dog titles and agility titles. Jag earned a Barn Hunt title. With my recent Flat-Coats, I've added advanced field titles as a goal. When I first wrote this, Gryffin had his Senior Hunter title, my first dog to earn any AKC hunt test titles, and my goal was to get all the way to Master. Having never attempted this title before, I was still overwhelmed by the requirements. Would we achieve that goal? I couldn't say at the time, but we were having a lot of fun aiming for it. Spoiler alert: Gryffin became my 1st CH OTCH Master Hunter and Sonic my 2nd.

Annual Goals
What titles and training goals do I hope to achieve in the next twelve months?

These goals tend to be more concrete. I have to look at what the rest of my life looks like for that time period and when I can attend trials. While we are blessed with a huge number of trials in my area (southeast Michigan), I don't like to trial every weekend, so I pick and choose dependent on several factors. These include host club, trial site, judges, and what other time commitments I have. I have a pretty good sense at this point in my training life when a dog is ready to qualify. It is always something of a gamble when we start to show a new dog - we are dealing with dogs, after all! I spend far more time training than trialing, and I look at trials as a test of our day-to-day training. When some error crops up once in a trial, I make note of it, but don't get too excited over it. But if it happens in another trial not long after, then it becomes more of a focus in my training. If a trial goes well, I think back over my recent training, review my training logs, and continue along that path. If I start having breakdowns in performance, I again return to my training logs to see if I can figure out the missing piece. I might focus on those particular exercises that didn't go well. I might also have to make a major course correction with a particular dog, which sometimes includes stopping showing for a stretch of time as we work to fix something that is causing us to fail a lot.

Monthly Goals
What do I need to do this month to advance toward our annual and life-time goals?

Some example monthly goals:
- Train in at least one new location each week
- Attend a fun match away from home
- Get started on Scent Discrimination

For the dogs I was training when I first wrote this, I was focusing on finishes with all three, and in a then-recent trial, I saw some excellent effort on finishes from each dog. Were they all perfect? Nope! But they were very much improved, and that's what I want to see.

Weekly Goals
What do I want to accomplish this week to advance my monthly goals?

I might pick 2-3 weaknesses for a given dog or in my handling and really focus in on those exercises or portions of exercises. In the advanced classes, there are several critical components: heeling, fronts, finishes, recall speed, jumping, retrieves, stays. You need to make sure that your foundation on each of these remains strong enough to satisfy your goals. I almost always work on some heeling when I have more than just a couple of minutes for training. This is the most important exercise for building and maintaining teamwork, and just like working out, it requires regular sessions for you and your dog to stay in tune with each other. Heeling is the exercise with the most difficult handling component – all that pesky footwork! – so you need to work on your part of the team as much as on your dog.

Occasionally in my advanced proofing classes, we make a list on a white board. Anyone who wants to join in writes their name and their dog's name on the list and includes 2-3 goals to focus on for the week. This is a voluntary thing, but usually those who participate make some good progress by doing this.

Many years ago, I stole an idea from Margie English. She described how she went about improving her dog's scores when she was working toward an OTCh title. She kept track of her dog's scores on each exercise in Open and Utility and then worked on the areas or exercise that were most consistent point-losers. Often the difference between winning or getting OTCh points is only .5 to 2 points, so if you can shave off that much, you are more likely to earn OTCh points. After showing my Border Terrier Java in both Open B and Utility B one weekend with so-so results, I did some calculations. We had to do 22 finishes over the 4 classes, and he lost a half point on all but 3 of the 22. I know this because I almost always go over my score sheet with the judge after the awards to be sure I know where we lost the points. So, we lost 9.5 points on just finishes over the course of the weekend. Sure enough, when he finally started being straight more often than crooked on his finishes, his scores went up enough that he finished his OTCh. My OTCh Australian Terrier Rio was the same way with fronts - once he started doing those more consistently, he finished his OTCh title.

✳ ✳ ✳

Now is the time to start thinking about what are realistic goals for you and your current dog(s), jot them down for later review, and get training.

5. TRAINING AND TRIAL LOGS

I have long been a record keeper when it comes to training and trialing my dogs. I do endeavor to write down our score breakdowns after every trial, including talking to the judges after the awards if possible, to get details of exactly where we lost points in their ring.

I also get every trial run videoed that I can. When I first wrote this article, I had just gotten an iPad, and switched to using that for 'taping' my runs. It meant I didn't have to take along my video camera, make sure the battery was charged, nor ensure I had a useable tape. The advent of tablets made the whole process of getting videoed vastly simpler.

Offer to video friends in return for having them video you. Having a video to review is such a help in catching mistakes, especially handler errors that you might be unaware of. Sometimes, my dogs shift some while I'm walking away on a recall. I was once videoing Sonic's early Drop on Recall training. When I reviewed the video, I discovered that she was lifting her butt and scooching forward several inches – she did it not just once, but multiple times! I was completely unaware of this error. The next day, I got the instructor in the class I was in to catch her making the error so I could correct it, and then also give her treats for staying put.

Another reason to get videoed is that it is grand to look back on a particularly memorable performance, especially years later when that dog is no longer with you. Some of my favorite memories of my first boy Flat-Coated Retriever Gryffin were some of his very creative NQs (non-qualifying performances). Having them on video probably helped me to remember them, and smile at the memories.

Some people like a paper log, some prefer something digital. I use both types, but I mostly use a digital log for my dog training, as I never run out of paper, which is a major stumbling block for me with paper logs.

When I got an app called 'Noteshelf' for the iPad, I started creating training log pages to use to keep track of our training and physical exercise endeavors. At that time, I made the log pages in a laborious way that fortunately isn't required anymore. Here is a blank one I was using for Ty's training. Ty was competing in Open B and Utility B, and we were mostly doing maintenance.

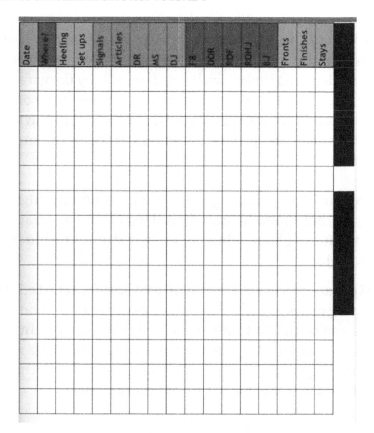

The following pictures show a couple of pages from Ty's log book, filled out in the Noteshelf app. I used the thumbs down icon to indicate that Ty went down on a sit stay. The highlighted circles were what I planned to do before I started training. Sometimes I would do all of them, sometimes I didn't. The ☐ was for proofing. The smiling and frowny faces were to show satisfying and unsatisfying work.

Date	Where?	Heeling	Ball work	Signals	Articles	DR	MS	DJ	FB	DOR	ROF	ROHJ	BJ	Fronts	Finishes	Stays	
30	B	✓	2@ 1m	👍				✓	Go outs		✓			✓	✓	✓	✓	N O V / D e C 2 O 1 1
1	B	✓		✓			✓	✓		✓			✓			✓	
6	B			✓						✓						✓	
7	B match	👍		✗	3's 3	✓	👍	👍	👍 👍		👍		✓			👍	
8	B	✓		✓	0's (+)						✓		✓			👍	
9	B	✓		✓		✓	🥄	✓		✓			🥄	🥄		👍	T Y
10	OTC CL	/		1	¹⁄₁	½	½	NQ		½	½	1	½			0⁄0	
10		196 in DB 12 om pts NQ in UB— 1ᴴ go out to sun spot															
11	OTC CL	½		½	½	1	½	1		0	½	0	½			NQ⁄0	
11		NQ in OB— blew 198.5 1ST place, HIT ☺				196 in UB 2ⁿᵈ place 11 orch pts!! 12 om pts												
12	LR															👍	
13	HW															👍	
14	HW	✓	2@ in (e)m	✓			✓									👎	
15	HW /B	✓		✓			✓	✓			✓	✓	✓	✓		👍	

Date	Where?	Heeling	Group	Signals	Articles	DR	MS	DJ	?B	UDR	UOF	UOHJ	EJ	Fronts	Finishes	Stays
16	B		P			✓	P		✓							👍
17																👍
18	B	✓	✓	5's S+7 d<11					P ↑3		✓					👍
19	B	✓	✓								✓					👍
20	H/B		✓											✓		👍
21	B	✓	✓												✓	👍
22	H														✓	
23	B	✓	👍	I's		✓	✓	✓	✓		✓					👍
24	B/H		✗			(bike ride + few circuit exs.)										👍
25				DAY OFF — MERRY Christmas												
26	AA DR	✓	✓	P	✓	P	✓				✓					👎
27	LA/B		P	P		P		P	✓							👎👎
29	Dental match	👍	👍	DND	3	✓	go over pro's	✓	✓	✓	✓	✓				👍
30	B	ring's 9's	✓			P		✓								👍

Something I noted from the 2nd filled out log is that I didn't do any special work on fronts in the week leading up to a set of trials, and that showed up in our ring performances. In order for our scores to nudge up enough to be in the placements, I needed to spend more time on them.

I had Ty checked in early January by my local rehab vet. In part because of my training log, I was able to tell the vet that Ty had gone down on sit stays 4 times in 2 days. In the past, when I haven't been training stays much, I've attributed the sit stay failures to that lack of practice. But I was doing them regularly and got thinking maybe it wasn't just a training issue. Sure enough, Ty had a sore triceps muscle. As my vet said, the triceps is an anti-gravity muscle, so it could certainly contribute to her lying down on her sit stays. Following a laser treatment by the vet, and home treatments by me, I was so proud of her qualifying in Open B both days at the trials the following weekend. She was doing a fair bit of front-foot shifting during the sit stay, but stayed upright.

With puppy Sonic, I had an obedience log and an 'other' log - for field related drills, conformation, and grooming. This helped me remember that it was time to trim her nails again (something I put off as long as possible with the big dogs). To this day, I have a grooming/nail trimming log for all my dogs.

The following pictures show Sonic's first 4 training log pages. The little TV and video camera icons were for days I took a video of her training.

Oct 2011 Log 1 Date	9	10	11	12	13	14	15	16	17	18
Name attention			✓	✓	✓	✓		✓		✓
Front attention					✓	✓	✓	✓	✓	
Metal article intro					✓	✓	✓	✓		
Play retrieve	✓	✓	✓	✓	✓	✓	✓	✓	✓	
Position changes	✓	✓ ✓	✓	✓	✓	✓	✓		✓	
Following outside	✓	✓		✓	✓	✓	✓			
Intro to leash	✓			✓		✓	✓	✓	✓	
Socializing/PK class	✓	✓		✓	✓	✓	✓		✓	
Restrained recalls		.		✓						
Cookie-toss recalls	✓ ✓	✓		✓				✓	✓	
Spin L + R	✓	✓	✓	✓		✓	✓		✓	✓
Swing finish L+R			✓ ✓	✓	✓	✓	✓			✓
Platform			✓	✓	✓		✓	✓	✓	✓
Sit + Maintain			✓	✓	✓	✓	✓ ✓	✓	✓	
Sit stay for meal						✓	✓	✓	✓	
Outings to a new place	✓	✓	✓ ✓		✓			✓		✓
Cookie-toss downs		✓	✓	📺	✓	✓	✓	📺	✓	✓
Wobble board				✓						
Grooming										
Vet visit		✓								
Chair fronts				✓				✓	✓ ✓	
Pat Nolan Targets		✓	✓ ✓		✓	✓	✓	✓	✓	✓
Stacking							✓	✓	✓	

Date	19	20	21	22	23	24	25	26	27	28
circle finch									📺	✓
Front attention		✓				📺			✓	
Cookie-toss down	✓	✓		✓		✓	✓	✓	✓	✓
Kick-back stand		✓		✓		📺				
P.N. Target work	✓			✓			✓	✓		
Following outside		✓	✓							
Find Heel		✓			📺		✓	✓		
Socializing/Outings	✓	✓	✓	✓	✓	✓	✓		✓	
Cookie-toss recals	✓	✓		✓	📺				✓	
Swing finish L & R		✓		✓		✓				
Sit and Maintain	✓			✓		📺		✓	✓	
Sit stay for meal	✓						✓		✓	✓
Chair fronts					✓	✓			📺	
Stacking		✓		✓	📷	✓	✓			✓
Platform fronts							✓	✓	📺	
Restrained recalls	✓									
Intro to db	✓	📺		✓		📺	✓			
Restraint Work			✓	✓	✓	✓	✓	✓	✓	
Toenails						✓			✓	
DB Lift						📺		✓		
Foot touch to target							📺			
Metal article									✓	
Back+forth gi-outs									✓	

✓

Date	31	1	2	3	4	5	6	7	8	9
Front attention	✓			✓	✓	✓	✓		✓	✓
[NEW] HP attention				✓	✓		✓		✓	✓
Cookie-toss down	✓			✓		✓		✓	✓	☝
Kick-back stand			✓		✓	✓	✓			✓	✓
Go-outs (target work)	✓		[TV]	✓		✓				[TV]
Find Heel	✓		[TV]	✓		✓		✓	✓	
Socializing/Outings			✓		PK		✓			✓
Cookie-toss recalls	✓			✓						
[NEW] CT recall thru chute				✓						✓
Swing finish L & R	✓	✓		✓	✓				✓	✓
Circle finish	✓		✓			✓		✓	✓	
Sit Stay	✓	✓				✓		✓		
[NEW] Scoot Sits			[TV]		✓	✓	✓		✓	[TV]
Chair fronts			✓			☝		✓		
Stacking	✓		✓	✓		[camera]		✓	✓	
Platform fronts	✓					head duck [NEW]			✓	
Restrained recalls			✓		✓	✓	✓			
Restraint work	✓	✓	✓		✓	✓		✓		✓
Toenails/Grooming			✓		✓			✓		☝
DB progression	✓	✓		✓	✓		✓	✓		
[NEW] Head holds				[TV]		✓		✓		
Perch work Foot touch		✓	✓	✓	PW	PW	[TV]	✓	✓	✓
[NEW] Back	[TV]	✓	✓		✓	✓	✓	☝	✓	[TV]

☝ = next step

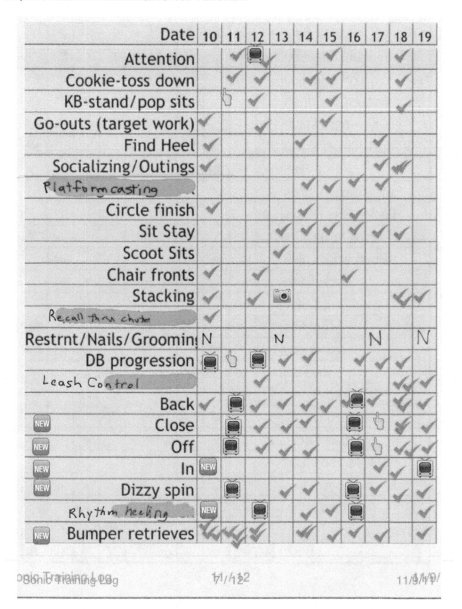

Date	10	11	12	13	14	15	16	17	18	19
Attention		✓	📺	✓			✓		✓	
Cookie-toss down		✓	✓		✓	✓			✓	
KB-stand/pop sits		👆	✓			✓			✓	
Go-outs (target work)	✓			✓		✓				
Find Heel	✓				✓			✓		
Socializing/Outings	✓							✓	✓	
Platform casting					✓	✓	✓	✓		
Circle finish	✓				✓		✓			
Sit Stay				✓	✓	✓	✓	✓	✓	
Scoot Sits				✓						
Chair fronts	✓		✓				✓			
Stacking	✓		✓	📷					✓	✓
Recall thru chute	✓									
Restrnt/Nails/Grooming	N			N				N		N
DB progression	📺	👆	📺	✓	✓		✓	✓	✓	
Leash Control			✓						✓	✓
Back	✓	📺	✓	✓	✓	✓	📺	✓	✓	✓
NEW Close		📺	✓	✓	✓		📺	👆	✓	✓
NEW Off		📺	✓	✓			📺	👆	✓	✓
NEW In NEW								✓	✓	📺
NEW Dizzy spin		📺		✓	✓		📺	✓	✓	✓
Rhythm heeling NEW			📺		✓	✓	📺		✓	
NEW Bumper retrieves	✓	✓	✓		✓	✓	✓	✓		✓

I seem to continue to fiddle with my training logs. This next

one is from Tigger's training log from early 2020. Some of the boxes, such as Signals in the middle of March, show a little triangle in them, which means I added a comment to that box for something particularly notable. I think I was keeping track of how many steps I could take, as I was still in the process of working out to full distance (about 16 steps). The double !! on Go outs were on days I used guides of some sort during go-out training. One feature about this type of log that I really like is being able to look quickly to see what I've worked on consistently vs. not at all or rarely.

																							March 2020			
16	19	21	22	23	24	25	26	27	29	1	2	4	5	6	7	8	9	11	16	17	18	19	20	22	23	24
▦	①	▦	③	①	▦	①				▦	③	①	▦	①	①	▦	②	②	①	①	①	①				
										×																
×	×														×								GO run-thru			
	×	×	×		×	✋				🐾	🐾	×	🐾	×	×	×	×	×		🐾	🐾	🐾				
	×		×									×	×		×	×		×	×		×		x	x		Drills
	×										🐾					🐾		×	×		×		x			
													×		×											
															×		✓		×				agil @ 12"			
			×	✓								×											x			
			×	✓								×											x			
						×							×						×							
		×		×	×					×	×	×	×					×	×		×		x		x	P
		×		×	×					×	×		×				🅿	×			×		x			
		×		×	×					🐾			×					×	×	×			x		x	
																					×		x			x
																					×		x			
											×		×						!! !!	!! !!	×	×	-			
											×		×						×	×	×	x	-			
		×		×	×					×	×						🐾	×	🐾		×	x			x	
																						×			x	
			×	×	×	×	🅿			×	×	×	×					🐾	×			x				
																			×	×	×	× x	X - #8 steps	13 steps		
																					×	x				
																							2x2 wvs			
×			×									×		×				×	×							

After watching Connie Cleveland's webinar on planning training sessions in the spring of 2020 after the pandemic shutdown, I created yet a different type of spreadsheet log to use for planning before training sessions. Since I was training all 4 of our dogs at least some, it really helped to keep track of what I was doing. I'd comment on how the dogs did as I went along.

4-30-2020

	Sonic		Jag		Tigger		Clipper	
Training order	3		4		2		1	
Tricks	Backups and spins at a distance	Improving	Down -> sit paws back	Okay	2 x 2's and channels	Closed 2x2's. Bit more. 100%.missing 1st or last pole a bunch on the channels		
Stationary Skills	Glove pivots	Bit better			Glove pivots	Improving		
Heeling Skills	Figure 8's	Nice	Figure 8's	Really nice	Figure 8's	Nice		
Recall Skills	Finishes	Ugh	Finishes	Over rotating just a bit on around. Quite good on swings.	Finishes	Quite nice		
Retrieve Skills	ROF	Good	ROF	Charging	ROF	√	2 sets of 4 tied together articles and my scented one	All good. Tied 4 used ones tp use next time as unscented .
Jumping Skills	ROHJ	Charging, nice fronts	ROHJ	Charging	ROHJ	√		

Trial Logs

I have dedicated Numbers spreadsheets to keep track of each of my dog's obedience trial records. I did it in an Excel spreadsheet for years, but the useful thing about the Numbers spreadsheets is the files are available on all of my devices (computer, iPad, iPhone). Numbers also allows easy use of fun icons, which makes it more enjoyable to use. Here is a blank daily trial log and one filled out for the weekend Tigger finished his CD. The spreadsheet is smart enough to calculate your final score if you put in the points you lost on each exercise. It isn't smart enough, though, to understand if you type in NQ for an exercise.

Club Name	
Show Site	
Travel time	
Date	

Class	Time	Judge	Class	Time	Judge

Exercise	Points off	Comments	Exercise	Points off	Comments

Total Pts Off		Total Pts Off	
Final Score		Final Score	
Placement		Placement	
Dogs competing		Dogs competing	
OTCh pts		OTCh pts	
OM pts		OM pts	
HIgh in trial		High Combined	

Club Name	Dayton DTC
Show Site	Their training building
Travel time	3+ hours
Date	1/4/20 & 1/5/20

Class	Time	Judge
Novice B	8:20	Charlotte Mietziner

Exercise	Points off	Comments
Heel on Leash and Fig 8	2.5	
SFE	0.0	
Heel Free	1.5	
Recall	0.5	
Sit stay get leash	0.0	
Stays	0.0	
Total Pts Off	4.5	
Final Score	195.5	
Placement	1st	
Dogs competing	6	
High in trial		

Class	Time	Judge
Novice B	8:20	Charlotte Mietziner

Exercise	Points off	Comments
Heel on Leash and Fig 8	2.0	
SFE	0.0	
Heel Free	1.5	
Recall	3.0	started to go to auto-finish. I got him to front. Requested finish was nice
Sit stay get leash	0.0	
Stays	0.0	
Total Pts Off	6.5	
Final Score	193.5	
Placement	2nd	
Dogs competing	7	
High Combined		

This next picture shows some of a worksheet with all of the exercise orders for all of the AKC's current classes in which I'm likely to show. When I start a new sheet for a given trial, I check at the Open B or Utility B ring to find out what order the judge has chosen for that day. I then copy the exercise order for that class order from this page and paste it into that day's log.

Class	Class	Class	Class	Class	Class	Class
Open B II	Open B III	Open B IV	Open B V	Open B VI	Utility A	Utility B I
Exercise	Exercise	Exercise	Exercise	Exercise	Exercise	Exercise
Broad Jump	Retrieve on Flat	Drop on Recall	Retrieve over High Jump	CD down stand sit	Signal Exercise	Signal Exercise
Retrieve over High Jump	Drop on Recall	Heel Free & Figure 8	Drop on Recall	Broad Jump	Scent Discrimination Article No. 1	Scent Discrimination Article No. 1
Retrieve on Flat	Retrieve over High Jump	Retrieve over High Jump	CD Stand sit down	Figure 8 & Heel Free	Scent Discrimination Article No. 2	Scent Discrimination Article No. 2
Drop on Recall	Broad Jump	CD down stand sit	Figure 8 & Heel Free	Drop on Recall	Directed Retrieve	Directed Retrieve
CD down, sit, stand	Figure 8 & Heel Free	Broad Jump	Retrieve on Flat	Retrieve over High Jump	Moving Stand and Examination	Moving Stand and Examination
Figure 8 & Heel Free	CD Stand sit down	Retrieve on Flat	Broad Jump	Retrieve on Flat	Directed Jumping	Directed Jumping
Stand stay get your leash	Stand stay get your leash	Stand stay get your leash	Stand stay get your leash	Stand stay get your leash		

This next picture shows my Border Terrier Jag's complete trial record for 2019 and the abbreviated 2020 trial season. I use this page to track OTCH and OM points, UDX legs, scores, NQs, and any special things of note – new titles, High in Trials, High Combined awards. It is great to have all the information in one place. I know some people keep a running total of average scores in a given class. There are many things you can do with the spreadsheet formulas if you choose to. I mostly just use the Sum function.

Trial	OM pts earned	Open score	Placement	Open pts	Utility score	placement	Utility pts	UDX leg	OTCh pts	Special event	Combined score
Gr Muskegon	9	192.5		9	-						
Kazoo	15	197.5	4th	15	NQ						
TKC sat	18	193		9	192		9	4th			385
TKC Sun	9	193		9	NQ						
OTCGL Sat	12	195.5	2nd	12	nq						
OTCGL Sun	0	NQ			NQ						
TOTAL 2018 591	0									32	
Dayton Sat	27	199	2nd	15	196	4th	12	5th		3 OM1	395
Dayton Sun	6	NQ				190.5	6				
TKC Fri	21	191.5	Auto fini	6	197.5	1st	15	6th		14	389
TKC Sun	21	191.5	Auto fini	6	197	4th	15	7th			388.5
Sportsman's Sat	15	190.5	Auto fini	6	192.5		9	8th			383
Sportsmen's Sun	9	194	Extra cor	9	NQ						-
Greater Brighton Collie Club	15	197	1st	15	NQ					2 HIT	-
Carolina Sat	0	NQ			NQ						-
Carolina Sun	0	NQ			NQ						-
GTOTC Sat	15	199	1st	15	NQ					6 HIT	-
GTOTC Sun	12	195.5		12	NQ						-
TCDTC SAT 1	15	197.5+	2nd	15	Nq						-
TCDTC Sat 2	0	-			NQ						-
TCDTC Sun	15	197		15	NQ						-
Holland MI KC	0	NQ			DNS						-
Gr Rapids KC	0	NQ			DNS						-
BTCA '19	6	NQ BJ, SGL			191.5	1st	6			OM2!	
AADTC Sat	27	198	1st	15	196	1st	12	9th	30	HIT, HCL	394
AADTC Sun	30	198	1st	15	197	1st	15	10th	34	HIT, HC, UDX, OTCH!!	395
MBGRC Sat	18	196		12	190		6	11th			386
MBCRC Sun	21	191		6	198.5	3rd	15	12th	3		389.5
Kazoo Fri	0	NQ CD			NQ DJ, Sig						
TKC Fri 11-22	9	NQ ROHJ			194.5		9				
TKC 11-23	30	197.5	3rd	15	198.5	3rd	15	13	5		396
TKC 11-24	30	197.5		15	197.5	2nd	15	14	8		395
OTCGL Sat	15	198.5	2nd	15	NQ SA1		-		1	OM3	
OTCGL Sun	24	195.5		12	196.5	3rd	12	15	1		392
TOTAL 2019 261	0									107	0
Dayton 1/4	12	196		12	NQ SA1&2		0				0
Dayton 1/5	12	196		12	NQ MS		0				0
TKC 2/7	15	197.5	3rd	15	NQ DR		0				
TKC 2/8	12	194.5		12	NQ drop, sa2		0	1			
TKC 2/8	24	197		15	194		9	16	1		391
Sportsmen's 2/22	12	195		12	188.5		0	17			383.5
Collie trial 2/29	12	NQ - stay on DOR			195	1st	12		10		
TOTAL 2019 99	0										0
	0										0
Totals	735			485			240		161		
OM1	200			140			60				
OM2	200			140			60				
OM3	200			125			75				
OM4	135			90			45				

Of course, I am a computer geek, so I love using my iPad for keeping track of so much of my dogs' training and trialing life.

I think it is very important as well as useful to keep detailed records of your training and trial results, and I recommend that you take these suggestions and develop a system that works best for you.

6. PRACTICE

A hallmark of talent is loving to practice. - Penelope Trunk, Brazen Careerist

An amateur practices until they get it right. A professional practices until they don't get it wrong. - Richard Crittenden (D.C. Opera Workshop)

Knowledge is of no value unless you put it into practice. - Anton Chekhov

While it matters a lot that you have a goal, a vision and an arc to get there, it matters even more that you don't skip the preliminary steps in your hurry to get to the future. Early steps might bore you, but miss even one and you might not get the chance to execute on the later ones. - Seth Godin, blog post 11/7/12

Field trial trainer Bill Hillman talks quite a bit about practice on his DVD *Retriever Training Fundamentals: Part 1 Land*. He argues that most trainers just don't practice enough with their dogs. They teach something a time or two, think the dog understands, and then move on to something else. Bill stresses continuing to practice the fundamental skills throughout a dog's lifetime.

I have loved puzzles and problem-solving since I was a child. Maybe it is why I liked math and computer programming so much when I was in school. I still love programming. I just love training dogs and people even more. I rode and trained horses as a teen, moving on to dogs in my early twenties. To me, dog training is one giant puzzle. Whether I am training for blind retrieves in the field or teaching my dog to heel with animation and precision for the obedience ring, it is critical to have an understanding of the training steps to follow. I have always believed that if one book or video on a topic is good, having six is better. I like getting a lot of different view-points on something. It helps me to study the road maps that other trainers follow and find success with. I like to see what they consider crucial foundation steps, and how they put them together into more complicated behaviors. If your foundation is weak, the later steps built on it will be weak. If your foundation is strong and well developed, the subsequent steps will usually be easier to teach.

An example of a critical foundation step is the *hold* when teaching a dog to retrieve. It is often the step that inexperienced trainers find the most difficult to master. Many dogs enjoy chewing and chomping on whatever is in their mouth, which means it is self-reinforcing. I have been guilty of glossing over this step to get to what appear to be sexier, more exciting steps. "Oh, look, my dog can race out to that dumbbell! He loves to grab it and race around with it, flipping it around in the air!" I was attending a summer field training workshop with Mitch White when my Flat-Coated Retriever Sonic was still fairly young. She had developed a bad habit of chomping on bumpers and I asked for help fixing it. Mitch introduces young retrievers to the hold using a leather glove on his right hand. It was not a technique I had used with prior dogs, and I hadn't used it with Sonic. When he asked why I hadn't done it with her, I think I replied something lame like, "I just didn't." When I got started with her son Tigger, I spent many weeks developing his hold, not only of my gloved hand, but of numerous different objects. When it came time to work on his force fetch, the solid hold made the whole process proceed faster, more smoothly, and with less stress for Tigger because we were able to concentrate on the taking of the items. He already knew how to hold.

Training one skill at a time is almost always the fastest approach. If you are struggling with an exercise with your dog, see if you can break it down more and practice smaller pieces. It rarely hurts to "go back to kindergarten" and review early steps.

Getting Guidance

It helps a lot to have an experienced instructor to help guide you along the training and skill-building road, especially when you are a new trainer and have never traveled *any* training road before. Sometimes that instructor is someone with whom you can take weekly classes. Sometimes it is someone who has written a book or produced a video on the topic. Sometimes it is a classmate who helps motivate you to train on a day when you are tired. But you still have to practice. No matter how great the instructor or book or DVD, if you don't practice the skills with your dog, you won't find success, whatever your definition of success is, whether it is to have a well-behaved companion in the home or a trial-winning obedience dog; a hunting companion or a Master Hunter.

Repetitions

Many dogs do very well with repetition, but others do not. Most dogs do require large amounts of repetitions of a skill before mastering it. If you have a dog who does not like repetition, you will likely be more successful if you change your focus exercise frequently during a training session. Perhaps you do 3-6 reps of skill A and then move on to skill B, skill C, etc. You then circle back and work on skill A again in the same training session.

Fluency

You might have heard or read about how many reps it takes to learn something, or how many hours you need to practice to gain mastery. Years ago, a google search about how many repetitions it took to master something led me to the article linked below, written by human educators. I found it so useful that I almost always start my competition obedience seminars by reading several short passages from the article, including:

> The real difference that we see in expert performers is that they behave fluently – both accurately and quickly, without hesitation.

and another one about foundation work:

> ...students in many educational programs often fail to achieve fluency. Instead, they progress by building one non-fluent skill on top of another until the whole skill set becomes 'top heavy' and falls apart.

> Even in relatively successful students, who do not falter in obvious ways, a lack of fluency in essential skills and knowledge can seriously limit their ability to achieve the full learning potential of which they are capable.

Here is a link to the full article if you are interested.

Planning Your Practice

When you are a "newbie" trainer, it can be easy to feel so overwhelmed about *what* to work on that you don't work on anything. Then there is the *how to* part of the equation. How do you teach your dog to do something? What do you do if your dog doesn't respond in the way the instructor's trained dog does? When I'm teaching my classes, I do skill demonstrations with my least experienced dog, or every so often, with a dog from the class. When I have a new puppy, that is who I am going to use in my earliest classes, because they are not polished, so will possibly make errors or at the least, look less fluent.

Here are the first two weeks of the practice guide I provide in the handouts for my Fundamentals course, which is my first competition obedience course.

Week 1

Power up clicker and/or special marker word by repeating it and immediately give a treat. Repeat 10-12 times. *Do one or two sessions only.*

Back Aways – 6-10 reps

Front & Center - 10-12 reps

Pass the cookie – 10-12 reps

Nose touch to hand – 6-10 reps

Find heel – 10-20 reps

Cookie-toss recalls – 6-10 reps

Perch/Platform – 6-10 reps

Week 2 – Add:

Front attention – 10 reps

Heel position attention – 10 reps

Stand -> down and down-> stand – 10 reps of each

Tug games – 15-30 seconds of play

When planning your training sessions, sometimes it is easy to focus on the skills that one or both of you especially enjoy or that your dog already does well. It can help to sandwich the more difficult skills in between easier or better-known ones.

Some dogs will do better with skill training every other day. Some thrive on multiple short sessions each day. You can really accomplish a lot in 5-10 minute sessions, especially if you have a plan.

It can be very useful to plan your next training session at the end of the current session, as you fill out your training log for the day. At that point, what went well and what needs more work is fresh in your mind.

* * *

What are you going to practice today?

7. DEVELOPING A CRITICAL EYE

I f you are like most people, when you start to train your first dog, you are tickled to get him to sit promptly on command. You might not notice that he takes a step or two backward every time he sits. We call this a **rock sit**. The problem with a rock sit in competition is that it can cause a dog that was in a good position before the sit to end up out of position after the sit. If the position is poor enough, you will lose points. But if no one has ever pointed out to you that a rock sit is A Thing, and why it is Something To Be Avoided, it is likely that you won't do anything to fix it, since you don't even know that it is something to be fixed. Sometimes rock sits are the result of the way you use food to teach your dog to sit, because you steer your dog backward into the sit. However, another possibility is that you have a breed of dog with a tendency to rock sit naturally. German Shepherd Dogs, Schnauzers of all sizes, Dalmatians, and many hounds are all breeds that I have seen rock sit.

I prefer dogs to **tuck sit** in competition. The dog keeps his front paws in place and tucks his rear forward as he sits. This will keep him in the same position after the sit as he was in before the sit. It is also more convenient in every-day life: you call your dog to you to attach a leash, so you want him close to you. If he rock-sits, he ends up sitting away from you, which might require you to step toward him. It can set up an annoying loop of dog rock sits > you step forward > dog backs away > you call him > he rock sits, etc.

How your dog sits is just one of a seemingly infinite number of details confronting a new trainer. Training for the competition ring, whatever the sport, is all about limiting errors that will lose you points. In obedience, there are errors that will cause you to NQ or non-qualify. Substantial errors are those that will lose you 3 or more points all at once, such as failure to sit on a halt. Minor errors are those for which you will lose ½ to 2 ½ points, depending on the severity.

How do you know what errors count as non-qualifying, substantial, or minor deductions? The very best way is to get a copy of the most recent regulations for the organization in which you want to earn titles, and then read it and reread it. I primarily do AKC events. The obedience regulations are available for free as a downloadable PDF on the AKC website, or for purchase for a nominal fee. I like the digital version, because I can easily search for something.

NQs

When I am gearing up for competition with a new dog, or moving up to a higher level with an experienced dog, I want to first eliminate, or at least minimize, errors that will cause us to NQ (non-qualify) in a trial. NQs are a fact of life for most of us who trial our dogs with any frequency. Many of my dogs have had one or two exercises that were particularly difficult for them to qualify on consistently. For my first dog, Australian Terrier Casey, the down on the Utility Signal exercise was her Achilles' heel. For my next dog, Flat-Coated Retriever Tramp, it was the Open B out of sight sit stay (she would frequently lay down). For my Border Terrier, Jag, it has been Scent Discrimination.

There is at least one element in every exercise in every class that is called the *principal part* of the exercise. If your dog fails to do that principal part, then you will fail, or NQ, that exercise and thus the class. On an obedience recall, coming before you call or failing to come on your first command is a fatal error for all levels except Beginner Novice, because those are both principal parts of the exercise.

Substantial Deductions

My next goal is to eliminate *substantial deductions*, which are errors that cost 3 or more points, but don't result in an NQ because they don't involve the principal part of the exercise. Some examples of a substantial deduction would be failing to move on a finish on your first cue or failing to sit at the end of the go-out in Utility.

If you want to earn a score in the 190s (out of a perfect 200 points) in obedience, you need to incur at most 1-2 substantial deductions. If you want to score 195 or higher, you should work to eliminate substantial deductions completely, as losing one big chunk of points all at once leaves very little room for other errors.

Minor Deductions

Minor deductions are those that are ½ to 2 ½ point deductions. In Rally, there are no ½ point deductions, so you and your dog don't need to be as precise to earn high scores. In Beginner Novice, there are ½ point deductions, but the scoring is more lenient than in the higher-level obedience classes.

Years ago, I coined a phrase, "minor halves vs. major halves" – e.g., a sit that was barely crooked vs. a sit that was clearly crooked, but both typically losing a ½ point. Judges do vary some in what they consider crooked enough to take a deduction. I judged Rally and Novice obedience for about 10 years, though never with great frequency. Like many new judges, I started out with "a sharp pencil", as exhibitors will say about a judge who tends to score teams with a more critical eye. After a weekend assignment in which

I judged Novice A & B, Beginner Novice and Rally, I was discussing my scoring in the Novice classes with another judge on the panel, and he teased me about being a tough scorer. That led me to have a conversation with one of the AKC Reps. She suggested that, given my level of experience in competing at the highest levels, perhaps my "eye" was more critical than judges without my level of experience; that perhaps I could adjust what I considered a ½ point deduction vs. a 1-point error, not being as quick to take a higher deduction. I think after that, I wasn't as tough when scoring.

Your Critical Eye

So, how do you develop your own critical eye? It certainly helps to have an instructor who has one, so she points out errors that you or your dog are making. As I said above, I work first on the most serious errors with both my own dogs and my students, gradually refining what I consider acceptable work from the dog. One important rule of training is to work on one thing at a time. Pick the big problem areas first.

As an instructor, I aim to avoid overwhelming my new students with too many details at once. Something I often say, particularly in my Fundamental class (my 1st level competition class): "If you have questions about why I am teaching you something, please ask, because it is generally leading to something more complicated, but I want to avoid overwhelming you with details."

Working in front of a mirror is a useful training tool, especially if you are working by yourself. Lacking a mirror at home, stores with big plate-glass windows can give you almost as useful information. This gives you a chance to see what you and your dog look like from the judge's point of view. I have several mirrors hanging on the walls in my training building. I use them a lot when I'm refining front sits, finishes, and halts on heeling. I like to use a mirror especially for sits in heel position, to help avoid twisting my upper body to the left to check the straightness of my dog's rear end.

If you have a smart phone or tablet, you most likely have a video camera app. Prop it up and train your dog in front of it. I started doing that when my Sonic was 8 weeks old, which led to numerous "Sonic videos" on YouTube. I continued this when my Border Terrier Jag came home and when I started training home-bred Tigger, though neither with quite the obsession I had with Sonic. When reviewing a just-taken video of my training, I often catch errors that one of us is making. Since I train alone a lot, this is a really valuable tool for me.

Although I never judged at the Open level, I did apprentice several times, which means sitting outside a ring, scoring each team in the class, and then reviewing those scores with the judge after the class is done. A point that was driven home for me via this experience was just how much where you are positioned when scoring a performance affects the final score. If you are watching a team heeling from the side vs. from in front or behind, you will catch different errors. Sitting outside the ring, often behind the handler's back on recalls, I couldn't see minor errors like mouthing the dumbbell or a dog nudging their handler with their nose on the front. But I could see a dog's rump flaring out on heeling or a handler stepping into her dog on an about turn, which is harder to see from the side. The AKC reps recommend varying your position when judging a heeling pattern, so you can see the team working from different sides.

To improve your ability to recognize smaller and smaller errors, it can be valuable to sit with an experienced exhibitor and watch teams in the obedience ring showing at the level you are preparing for. Have her point out errors to you and the likely point deduction for those errors. Lacking the in-person trial experience, you can find a seemingly infinite number of performances at all levels on YouTube. You can do the same analysis of these video performances.

The more your critical eye improves, the quicker you will get at catching your dog making errors so you can interrupt them. A major error I often see in classes and the trial ring is a dog that is doing "auto finishes" – the dog skips sitting in front and automatically goes right to heel position. This is typically a 5-point deduction and therefore a huge hit on your score, especially in the Open and Utility classes, which have lots of fronts. Inexperienced trainers often do nothing in training when their dog starts to run past instead of stopping in front. I've even seen trainers look up at the ceiling when their dog zooms around them. This tells me that handler knows it is a problem. This ceiling glancing is going to do nothing to fix this costly error! At the very least, I mark the error with my verbal correction marker and rotate my position to prevent my dog from completing the finish. If he is going to my right, I rotate to my right (clockwise). I'll put out a foot or hand to block him from continuing. Sometimes, your dog starts to go directly to heel automatically because you are giving treats far more often for finishes than for fronts. You need to even out which "balance point" you are reinforcing. Any time your dog is anticipating a given step in a sequence, i.e., a *balance point*, you need to reinforce the previous step in the sequence more often. If your dog is coming before you call him on a recall, you need to reinforce the sit stay.

Another serious error is a dog who is sniffing the floor. If your dog is getting his nose all the way down to the floor before you respond, you are reacting much too slowly to his loss of attention. I want to react the instant his head drops from the heads-up position I train for. When just getting started on teaching heeling to a new puppy, I respond to a head drop by stopping. If it happens a lot, I reduce how many steps I expect him to take before reinforcing. Sometimes, it means only asking for 1-3 steps.

When training a young dog, I much prefer to "catch him being right" instead of having to correct him for being wrong. Your critical eye is just as important for catching correct responses as for stopping incorrect ones.

If you are not usually a detail-oriented person, your critical eye may take more time to develop. You may also not really care to develop it to a super-refined level. That is one of my favorite parts of obedience: you can earn a lot of titles without having to be perfect. In fact, there are very, very few perfect 200 scores earned each year. But if your goal is to raise your scores, working on your critical eye is going to help you achieve that goal.

8. THE CARE AND FEEDING OF A TRAINING PARTNER

What is a training partner? It is someone with whom you can get together regularly to train your dogs. It is someone with whom you can talk over training issues. It helps if your TP has a similar schedule to you, so it isn't too hard to find time to meet. Having similar long-term goals is helpful, though not critical. It will help you a lot if your TP is more experienced than you are, because you will be able to learn a lot from her. Those of us who have been doing this for a long time enjoy seeing new trainers getting hooked on the sport we have loved for so many years. But it doesn't have to be someone more experienced. I continue to learn from new trainers. Sometimes, because of no preconceived ideas, new trainers come up with fabulous "think outside the box" solutions for problems that experienced trainers don't.

Having dogs at similar levels is another benefit, because you'll need the same equipment for training, and you can each supply some. It means you can go to trials together and cheer each other on, or commiserate on the days it doesn't go so well. For many of us, the social aspect of dog competitions is a large part of the fun. Of course, even if you aren't at the same level, most trials have classes of many different levels going on, so you can still go to shows together.

Finding a Training Partner

Where should you look for a training partner? If you are taking a class somewhere, ask your classmates if they would be interested in meeting outside of class to practice together. It makes you more likely to do your homework and it simply makes it more fun. You can help each other by calling commands if the dogs are advanced enough; doing stand for exams; putting out scent articles; holding a young dog for recalls. Sometimes it is helpful to simply train alongside each other, but it is even better if you can take the time to play "judge" and provide direct distractions for each other for at least part of your time together. This also gives your dog a chance to practice being quiet in his crate while you are doing something else.

Another potential place to look is at a local dog club. Even if it isn't an obedience club, you might find someone interested in obedience training who belongs to an agility club or a conformation club. Attend nearby obedience trials and matches and watch people. Look for someone whose dog works like you wish yours would. Ask them where they train. If you are already competing with your dog for titles, find out where your fellow exhibitors live. Addresses are usually listed in the back of the trial catalog.

It is also very helpful to find someone who is as dedicated to training as you are. There are times that I just don't feel very motivated to train my dogs, but knowing that I'm meeting up with someone gets me out the door. I am almost always glad that I went and trained, and my dogs love road trips.

These days, it is also possible to find training partners on line. There are groups for any kind of activity you can imagine on Facebook and other social media sites. Join some of those. They are great resources for people all over the country. With the increased familiarity with Zoom and other such video platforms with so many people now working from home, you might be able to find a virtual training partner who you can meet up with via a weekly Zoom call.

I am blessed to live in a highly active dog training community, with many opportunities within a 2-hour radius of Ann Arbor. I once met a friend who lives outside of Chicago (which means we are 5 hours apart) at another friend's training building that is about 1/2 way between Ann Arbor and Chicago. It took three different attempts before the winter weather cooperated, but it was well worth the effort and we had a lot of fun.

Preparing for Tournaments

There are a lot of trainers in my general area of the Midwest who get invited to attend the AKC's NOC (National Obedience Championship) tournament each year. We have gotten together for many years to help each other prepare for the event. The NOC is structured very differently than the typical obedience trial, with each team going into the ring 6-8 times a day, performing 2-4 exercises from both Open and Utility. The teams rotate around from ring to ring, starting at 8:00 AM and continuing until 5:00 PM in some cases. It is a long and physically exhausting day for both dogs and humans, and we work on reproducing this, albeit on a smaller scale, when we do our NOC training days. I've been lucky enough to participate in these training days in at least 5 different training facilities over the many years I've been attending the NOC. Usually, we take turns alternating working our dog with playing judge and steward. The last one that I organized was held in the Ann Arbor Dog Training Club's beautiful and HUGE new performance building, in which the club holds one-ring agility trials. We had three rings arranged in a T, to provide distractions similar to what we would see at the big event. We also had dedicated judges and stewards for each ring, each set working a half-day shift. This made the day so much smoother for those of us working our dogs. During our break to eat our potluck lunch, the workers trained their own dogs. Some of them wanted run throughs. Others just wished to work their dog in the environment. It was such a fun day! The new facility was incredibly wonderful as a venue for such a training day. Everyone participating paid a nominal fee to cover the rental fee charged by the club.

*　*　*

In thinking back over the many training partners I've had over the 30+ years I've been training, I think fondly of the friendships, the hours and hours spent training and problem solving, and the thrill of victory, not just for myself but also for them.

If you don't already have one, I encourage you to find someone to train with. I don't think you'll be sorry.

9. FOOD DELAY

One of the biggest hurdles for many trainers who use food to train their dogs is weaning off the food sufficiently to get reliable obedience ring performances from their dogs. I think I first heard the term *Food Delay* in one of Dawn Jecs' books. I want to describe at least some of the ways in which I work on this process with my dogs.

When I first introduce an exercise, I often have treats in sight in my hands, and use the treats as a lure or magnet. When working with my dog in heel position, I typically hold a single treat in my left hand, with several in my right hand for easy reloading of my left hand. I start out with a one-to-one ratio of action to CR (conditioned reinforcer or marker word) and treat. My first step in the weaning process is to increase the number of repetitions my dog must do or the duration of such exercises as attention, heeling, or stays, with the food readily visible. As my dog's understanding grows, I raise the ratio to two to six correct responses per CR/treat, still occasionally treating two in a row.

The next step is to hide the treats in a closed fist, building from a single repetition to two to six per treat. When I can get several responses in a row with treats hidden in my hands, I give a treat on the last one of the series, and with empty hands, I ask for one more repetition. I use all of the other cues I was using when the food was there, such as hand position and leash pressure. After a single response, I CR and I give my dog a treat from my pocket. My dog needs to do many repetitions when the food is obvious and a single one when it is not.

I gradually reduce not just the visible food cues, but also any other extra cues I'm using, such as leash pressure and extraneous hand cues. I am striving to have my dogs respond to a single cue, either a verbal command or a non-verbal signal. Most dogs learn via successful repetition, and lots of it. If you have a dog for whom repetition either bores him or confuses him, you will need to spread your reps out over more training sessions.

What is Food Delay?

Food Delay is the process of working your dog with no physical reinforcers - food or a toy - in your hands, in your pocket, in your mouth, or tucked under your shirt. In short, you must get it *all* off your person. If your dog has been very used to food and/or a toy always being readily present, you might discover these are part of your dog's cueing system that you were unaware of.

Before I start the Food Delay exercise, my dog should have a good understanding of my *Find Heel* exercise, including distraction resistance. If you aren't familiar with this, take a look at these videos:

Find heel 1

Find heel 2

I spend several months teaching my dog all the different components of heeling – Rhythm Heeling, pace changes, turns, halts, and Figure 8's, but I return to Find Heel when I start Food Delay.

Getting Started with Food Delay

I'm going to describe a formula of food on you and food off you, but it is critical that you do not do this exactly this way more than a couple of times in a row. Let me repeat: *do not do this exact formula more than a time or two.* Dogs are very good at counting, so you need to be more random than that.

After you have removed all reinforcers from your pockets, etc. - take that bait bag off! – place nine treats on a spot too high for your dog to reach, such as a counter or windowsill. One time, when I was demonstrating this exercise with Sonic at a weekend seminar, I put my treats on a table, from which naughty Sonic immediately stole several treats. It got a big laugh from the attendees, and served as an example of what not to do.

Leave six of your nine treats on the counter, and begin your Find Heel work. The first three times your dog gets to heel position, CR and treat him. You may start with a treat in your left hand, but be aware you want to become more subtle about it before you are done teaching this skill. After giving the third treat, continue walking without making any fanfare that you have no food on you. When your dog catches up again, CR, and with a phrase such as "Let's go get a cookie!", run or walk briskly to your treat stash. Give him one, and leave empty handed. Some dogs like to hang out near the treat supply, which is why it is critical you put them somewhere your dog can't steal them. It's almost as though the dog is saying, "Hey, dummy, the treats are *here!*" Repeat this 'dog catches up, CR, "let's go get a cookie!"' routine two more times, which has now used up three more treats. Take the remaining treats with you, and finish up by rewarding him directly for catching up three more times.

So now you've done this formula of *three on–three off–three on* once. The next time you work Food Delay, you need to change the formula some, such as *two on–one off–one on–two off–three on*. Plan to work on a ratio of *two treats on you to one treat off* for a while, but be as random about it as you can be. It can also be important with certain too-clever critters that you are subtle about when you take extra treats with you vs. when you leave empty handed. You can do this by tossing a treat for the dog to chase while you reload (or don't) vs. simply delivering a treat directly and then reloading (or not).

Building Duration

As you practice this, start requiring your dog to heel with you for longer periods of time before you deliver a treat or run to your stash of treats. This starts with just a few steps after your dog arrives in heel position. Over time, you will want to work your way up to an entire ring performance for a jackpot at the end.

You can do a similar exercise using a special toy instead of food. I practice with a toy on the floor to which I release my dog when he is concentrating and performing a given exercise well enough. Here is a link to a video of Sonic training with a toy on the floor for the first time when she was 5.5 months old.

Food Delay is critically important to start teaching early. You don't want the lack of food in your hands to turn a switch off in your dog's head. Start early and practice it often!

10. TRAINING WITH LIMITED SPACE OR TIME

With the onset of cold and wintery weather here in the north, many people have limited training time because of darkness and bad weather. While I have the luxury of space because I have a training building in my back yard, I don't always have the luxury of a lot of time for training. I'd like to discuss how I spend that limited time to make progress toward my goals with my own dogs.

If there is room to do so, I work on heeling. Even if I only have a few minutes, I can work on building my teamwork with my dog by doing what I call *Rhythm Heeling* - moving with my dog at a consistent and brisk rhythm, with the dog's attention on me, and maintaining a consistent position at my left side, i.e., heel position. I still use a metronome sometimes, set at 124 steps per minute for my Flat-Coated Retrievers, and 119 or so for my Border Terrier. When there is enough space, we heel in big flowing circles, just clockwise to the right with an inexperienced dog, in either direction for a more experienced dog. When my experienced dog is working well with me - maintaining attention, position, and rhythm, I might add some turns, smaller circles, pace changes, and halts. With my green dog, I don't put these elements together until he can "do" Rhythm Heeling consistently well. I work on the components that will become turns, halts, and pace changes separately. I use the Rhythm Heeling exercise to limber up both me and my dog before we enter the ring at a trial.

When space is limited, I work on what used to be called doodling. I've referred to doodling as Maneuvers for years, and it's now called Rally :-). Doodling consists of pivots to the left and right of varying degrees; side-stepping left and right; backing up; working on fronts in several ways; working on your dog getting himself to a sit in heel position, AKA a set up; and finishes.

The reality for most trainers is that their dog is going to do some lousy, though qualifying, fronts in the trial ring: positions such as lying down in front of you, sitting sideways off your right hip, or standing an arm's length in front of you. To prepare for this, I recommend that you practice finishes with your dog starting in all sorts of oddball but qualifying locations around you. This is a drill we occasionally work on in my advanced classes. Put your dog in a sit, down, or stand, then adjust your position to the dog to be less than ideal. Cue your finish. Does your dog respond correctly to your command, or fix his front position? If you've had a really poor front, it is good to know that you can salvage the points for the finish because you've trained for this contingency.

When I first wrote this, I was working on front position maneuvers with Ty, my then-youngest dog, with a dumbbell in her mouth. She was showing definite signs of improvement, but she was just beginning to remember to hold the dumbbell without mouthing while she did the small position shifts I asked her to do. She could do these minor shifts beautifully when her mouth was empty. When we added in holding her dumbbell, it was much harder for her.

In a hallway, you can work on:
    Short recalls
    Position changes at a distance (verbal or signal) needed for the Open Command Discrimination exercise, the Utility Signal Exercise, and several of the Excellent and Master Rally

signs
A variety of retrieve-related skills:
    Beginning retrieving work
    Dumbbell retrieves
    Glove retrieves with different turns before the retrieve
    Scent articles
Go-outs
About turns
A series of quick halts
Moving stands
Stays
Fronts
Finishes

You can teach your dog to touch a target with his nose or a front paw. You can use this later for working on go-outs or the broad jump. You can proof your dog's dumbbell pickup by placing it near a distraction, such as a toy or something that looks like food but isn't. You can also work on skills for many of the Rally signs, even without having signs out.

You can simply practice your shaping skills by playing Karen Pryor's "101 things to do with a box" game, where you put a cardboard box in the center of a room and click and treat your dog for interacting with it in a different way each training session. I played the game a lot with my first Border Terrier Java. He would circle the box, jump in the box and sit, jump in and immediately jump out again, jump on the upside-down box, put front paws up on the side of the box, dig in a corner once inside the box... He was very creative!

Do you have a big island in your kitchen? Or a formal dining room that is collecting dust? Move any chairs out of the way and heel rectangles around the island or table, which will help your dog make tight left turns.

Do you have an office chair on wheels? You can use it to do multiple moving chair fronts, like scoot fronts. For a stationary chair front, you sit with your feet extended in front of you, and guide your dog to sit between your legs to help him learn to sit straight. After each sit, you toss a treat behind your dog to start over.

When you sit in a rolling chair, you push yourself backward a few inches after each sit, and have your dog move with you and sit again. When you run out of space, toss a cookie behind your dog, scoot yourself back across the room, and start over. It's pretty fun!

You can work on various tricks that help to build your dog's strength and flexibility, such as sitting up/begging, waving, doing figure 8's around your legs, rolling over, and spinning to the left and right.

If your dog is too perfect at home, talk to a friend who also trains, and go train at her house. Invite her over to your house the next time. Sometimes just adding another dog around will cause your dog to be less than perfect at home.

I've heard short training sessions called *Flash Sessions* – 3-5 minute long sessions to work on one skill. You grab a few treats and your dog and do several reps of a single skill. You might do multiple Flash Sessions in a day, which can add up to a solid quantity of training over the course of a week. My writing partner Judy Byron referred to these as "cheese and carrots" training, which she did in her kitchen when she was preparing a meal.

* * *

Be creative with your limited time and space and have fun with your dog.

11. HOW TO FIT A DOG FOR A DUMBBELL

Before I start measuring a dog for a dumbbell, I like to ensure that he has had some solid training on taking the dumbbell and holding it, even if only for a few seconds. I do not want a dog's first experience with a dumbbell to involve some stranger (me) shoving something in their mouth and holding their muzzle for as long as it takes to evaluate the fit. This is a recipe for a lot of problems! I have a large collection of varied-sized dumbbells, so I almost always have one that is a close-enough fit that a student can borrow to get started. You don't need a perfectly fitting dumbbell to begin training the retrieve.

This link is video extracted from *Totally Fetching: Teaching and Proofing a Reliable Retrieve,* my DVD on how I teach and proof the retrieve. You will see a variety of dogs holding both properly-fitted and improperly-fitted dumbbells.

Dumbbell Elements

There are three elements to consider when fitting a dumbbell to your dog: the height of the bells, the thickness of the dowel, and the width between the bells.

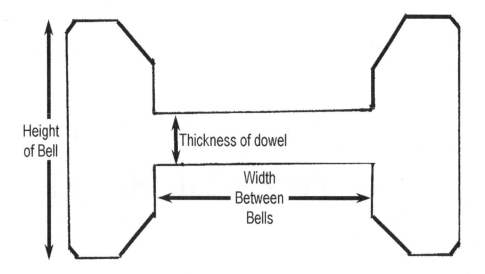

Many dumbbells are made with tapered bells to allow for a more comfortable fit. An "off-the-shelf" size is fine for many dogs, but some breeds require a custom fit due to their unusual length or width of muzzle. This includes dogs with very long and narrow muzzles, such as Shelties and Belgians, or dogs with very little muzzle length, such as Pugs and Brussels Griffons.

The ideal placement of the dumbbell is directly behind the canine teeth. Your dog should hold it firmly. I like the bells of the dumbbell to rest gently against the dog's lips. I don't want to see any gaps between the bell and the dog's lips. Such gaps make it easier for the dog to roll the dumbbell back onto his molars, which usually leads to mouthing or worse, chewing and chomping. If there is too little space between the bells, your dog's lips can get pinched, causing discomfort, which would likely reduce his desire to take it.

If the bells are too large, they can interfere with your dog's vision. If they are too small, your dog may have difficulty picking the dumbbell up smoothly without hitting his nose on the ground.

A thicker dowel can help prevent your dog from rolling the dumbbell to the back of his mouth. You want him to be able to clench the dowel comfortably. It is possible for your dog to roll a thin-doweled dumbbell even when his teeth are closed tightly. Also, a thin dowel on a wooden dumbbell tends to break easily.

From the AKC Obedience Regulations:

> The dumbbell, which must be approved by the judge, will be made of one or more solid pieces of wood or non-wooden material similar in size, shape and weight to a wooden dumbbell. Metal dumbbells are not permitted. Dumbbells will not be hollowed out. They may be unfinished, coated with a clear finish or may be any color. They may not have attachments but may display the person's name, the dog's call name, and/or the dog's picture (or insignia). Titles may not be displayed. The size of the dumbbell will be proportionate to the size of the dog.

When I first started competing in obedience, dumbbells typically had white ends. You are now allowed to use colored dumbbells, and I have a lot of friends and students who use non-white-ended dumbbells. I still prefer to use those with white ends, as I think they show up best on the surfaces on which I typically train and trial. I like the contrast the white ends provide for dark surfaces.

I get my custom-made wooden dumbbells from Phillip Klosinski of Toledo, OH. I've measured a lot of dogs all around the country with the spiffy dumbbell measuring kit Phil gave me years ago. The kit has a large variety of end sizes with different dowel thicknesses. One end is fixed and the other one can slide. The kit has proven itself very useful over the years. If you use the link above, which will create an email addressed to him, supply him with measurements in this order:

> Height of bell X dowel thickness X width between the bells
> For example: 3" X 5/8" X 2.5"

To measure a dog with my measuring kit, I choose an end size that I think is approximately right. For my Flat-Coated Retrievers, I typically pick a 3" bell height, with a 5/8" dowel thickness, and 2.5" between the bells. Golden Retrievers often have somewhat wider muzzles, so I'd start with the same bell height and dowel thickness, but widen the width out to 2.75". My Border Terrier uses a bell height of 2", with 1.75" between the bells.

If the dog I'm measuring will already pick up a dumbbell, I have the owner try out the new size to see if it is an improvement over the size they've been using.

To get an approximate measurement for a dumbbell with which to get started, take a pencil, pen, or thin dowel. If your dog will take the pencil and hold it, slide it forward just behind his canine teeth, and close your hands around it on either side of your dog's muzzle, snug up against his lips. If he won't hold it yet, work to get him to rest his chin on the pencil, again snugging your fists up on either side of his muzzle. Measure the distance between your fists with a ruler. That is the width. Dumbbell suppliers can usually guide you pretty accurately on the other sizes if you supply the breed of dog and width of muzzle.

While I mostly use wooden dumbbells, I do use a plastic one with my Border Terrier Jag, purchased from Max200. I like the way the ends are tapered for his muzzle shape. J & J Dog Supplies is another longtime supplier of obedience equipment.

Often, when I see a student struggling with a particular aspect of teaching their dog the retrieve, a change in dumbbell size can dramatically reduce the issue. If your dog is picking up his dumbbell by the end, or ending up with it somewhat diagonally in his mouth, a taller bell size can reduce both of those problems, because it makes the bar of the dumbbell more inviting for him to grab.

Some dogs love chewing on wood so much that a switch to a plastic dumbbell can greatly reduce that desire to chew. I once had a student whose Labrador Retriever spun and chewed her wooden dumbbell so much that the bar broke in pieces within about a week!

Are you interested in ordering a copy of Totally Fetching: Teaching and Proofing a Reliable Retrieve DVD? See the NDT website to do so.

12. AKC OBEDIENCE NUMBERS QUIZ

I am something of a numbers geek. When I first created this quiz, I was rather surprised at how many numbers there are related to setting up a ring, such as how far you need to stand from jumps, the distance between objects, such as Figure 8 posts, Utility gloves and articles, etc. I also found that many of my students didn't keep it in their head that the Utility jumps are to be set up a certain distance from the end opposite the end with the stewards table, or that the jumps should be a specified distance apart, or that where they stood by the broad jump was important.

I've turned the original quiz into a Google form which will automatically grade you. I hope you try it out and test your knowledge.

TAKE THE QUIZ

ABOUT THE AUTHOR

I have titled eleven dogs, six Flat-Coated Retrievers and five terriers, ten of them to the UD level so far, and earned seven OTCH titles: four on Flat-Coats, one on an Australian Terrier (the breed's first), and two on Border Terriers. I have earned numerous High In Trial and High Combined awards, as well as tournament placements over my 30+ year obedience career.

My ninth dog, Flat-Coated Retriever Sonic, who was forced into retirement by the pandemic, ended her career as **Ch OTCh Coastalight Prime Time UDX4 OM7 RE MH WCX.**

My tenth dog, Border Terrier Jag (**GCh OTCh Riverside Jaguar UDX OM3 BN GN RE NA NAJ RATN**), like Sonic, went from CD to UD in 12 months. In the fall of 2019, in what was probably the best four-month period in my trial career, Jag finished his OTCh and UDX titles just nine days after Sonic finished her OTCh.

Tigger (**Ch Northfield Quantum Leap CD PCD RM SH WCX**), Sonic's son, finished his CD in January 2020 and one leg on his CDX before the pandemic shutdown. He finished his breed championship entirely out of the Bred-By Exhibitor class, which made me very proud. He earned 2nd place in the Advanced Division at the 2018 Rally National Championship.

I have competed at the AKC National Obedience Invitational/ National Obedience Championship 8 times, including the first two in 1995 and 1996, and have been invited several more times. I placed in the Terrier group with two different dogs (Rio and Java) and most recently made it to the top 50 with Sonic in 2018. Both Sonic and Jag were invited to the 2020 NOC, but the pandemic caused us to stay home. I have also competed with my dogs in conformation, rally, agility, tracking, barn hunt, and hunt tests, reaching the Master level with my first hunt test dog, Gryffin and more recently with Sonic.

I am the co-author of the book *Competition Obedience: A Balancing Act (1998)* with Judy Byron (who passed away in 2000), and the video *Positively Fetching: Teaching the Obedience Retrieves Using Food (1995)*. My most recent book was *The Art of Proofing: Preparing Your Dog for Obedience Trials (2008)*. In January 2011, I released an updated version of the retrieve video on DVD, and renamed it *Totally Fetching: Teaching and Proofing a Reliable Retrieve.*

I was an AKC Rally and Novice Obedience Judge for about ten years (now retired) and served on the 2007 AKC Obedience Advisory Committee.

I have been an obedience instructor since 1988 when I started teaching classes at the local Ann Arbor Dog Training Club. I opened my training school Northfield Dog Training in 1990. I have taught classes from puppy through Utility, Rally, and the occasional Intro to Retrieving for field dogs. My classes are made up of dogs from a large variety of breeds, from toys to giants. I really enjoy helping people learn the details that make up competition obedience and Rally. I have also been teaching 2-day obedience training seminars around North America since my first one sometime in the 1990's.

In 2016, Sonic whelped my first-ever litter of puppies. She had her second litter in 2018. It was a *lot* of time-consuming work but very gratifying. We kept Tigger from the first litter, and Clipper (**Northfield Total Eclipse of the Moon RI WC**) from the second. Clipper has become my husband Fritz's devoted companion, and they have so far earned several Rally titles, his first time ever earning titles.

In late December 2020, I started a program I call COPS, which stands for *competition obedience practice sessions*. People can either join me on a Zoom call or watch a video replay later of me training one of my dogs on a set of skills that vary from day to day. The participants can train their dog along with me. I started it as a way to motivate me to train my own neglected dogs, and people seem to be enjoying it and getting motivated to work their own dogs. The program is very much in its infancy right now, but if you are interested in learning more, see the COPS Facebook page.

With the 2020 pandemic causing me to shut down my indoor in-person training, I turned to getting on-line. I created *Maneuvers On-Line,* which is an on-line video-based training course in which I teach my favorite-to-teach skills, Maneuvers. Judy Byron and I called this set of skills "Power Steering" in *Competition Obedience: A Balancing Act.* I am continuing to develop other on-line courses.

Fritz and I have two adult sons, Chris and Ryan. Fritz retired in May 2020 after a 40-year career in software programming. With the sudden availability of lots more time caused by the shuttering of most of my training business, plus the food uncertainty due to the pandemic, I jumped back into having a huge vegetable garden, something which brought me a lot of joy in an uncertain time.

Fritz was a devoted runner before we met, running cross-country in high school and college, and running several marathons. His devotion to his running has long been a motivator for me, and we've really upped our fitness regimen in the past year, running in several virtual 5K and 10K races. Clipper and Tigger are both great running companions, and all four dogs love the regular walks on our property and on the country roads near our house on our non-running days.

I have also sung in a women's chorus since 1990, though it is another activity interrupted by the pandemic. I look forward to returning to that in the future.

Photo by Cathi Winkles Photography

BOOKS BY THIS AUTHOR

Competition Obedience: A Balancing Act

In 1998, Judy Byron and Adele Yunck released this nearly 400 page book on training dogs for competition obedience using conditioned reinforcers, food, and fair corrections. It covers all aspects of training, from picking a puppy, training him in the foundation exercises, and proceeding from Novice through Utility training. While Adele and Judy trained in many similar ways, they also describe many of the ways their training toolbox differed. Judy and Adele wrote the book to help trainers who live in remote places without access to good training classes. The book has helped numerous trainers achieve advanced titles with their dogs. The book is liberally illustrated with photos, drawings, and diagrams, and has a very thorough index, helping you to find what you need to work on quickly.

The book:
* Discusses a balanced approach to training, using both positive and negative reinforcement, with a focus on the use of conditioned reinforcers.
* Contains more than 200 illustrations and photos that highlight the text.
* Includes a detailed, 14 page index.
* Provides many ideas for proofing for the ring.

Describes how to:

* Choose the right puppy for obedience.
* Teach a solid foundation for all of the AKC Novice, Open and Utility exercises.
* Wean off food for the ring.
* Know when you are ready to show.

The Art Of Proofing:
Preparing Your Dog For Obedience Trials

"Proofing is a test. When you proof an exercise with your dog, you are testing his understanding of that exercise under increasingly difficult levels of distractions. Through proofing, you want to increase your dog's ability to ignore distractions and stay focused on you or the current exercise. When he does get distracted, you want him to get back on task promptly. If you do it properly, proofing builds confidence rather than eroding it." - pg. 3, The Art of Proofing"

In 2008, Adele Yunck self-published this handy little spiral-bound book. It is chock full of ideas for proofing your dog in preparation for obedience and rally trial competition. It gives ideas for proofing in a group setting like a training class, with one helper, and when you are by yourself. The book is liberally illustrated with photos, drawings, and diagrams, and has a thorough index, helping you to find what you need to work on quickly.

Totally Fetching:
Teaching And Proofing A Reliable Retrieve Dvd

In 1995, Adele Yunck and Judy Byron released a 60-minute VHS tape called Positively Fetching: Teaching the Obedience Retrieves Using Food. The video showed how to teach a dog to retrieve a dumbbell and the other items needed for the competition obedience ring, starting with picking appropriate equipment, and taking trainers through each step of the process required to teach a dog to retrieve. Many competitors have mastered this sometimes-difficult concept and gone on to earn advanced titles with their dog, with help from the original tape.

In early 2010, Adele released an updated version on DVD, keeping the best of the original footage, replacing some parts, and adding about 10 minutes of new material. This new material includes a technique for improving the Hold and demonstrations of proofing steps.

Included in the purchase is a small booklet containing the narration of the video for quick reference when out training.

Made in United States
North Haven, CT
26 November 2023

44581169R00049